D0952807

TEAMWORKS!

TEAMWORKS!

TEAMWORKS!

Building Support Groups That Guarantee Success

BARBARA SHER and ANNIE GOTTLIEB

WARNER BOOKS

A Warner Communications Company

Copyright © 1989 by Barbara Sher and Annie Gottlieb
All rights reserved.

Warner Books, Inc., 666 Fifth Avenue, New York, NY 10103

W A Warner Communications Company

Printed in the United States of America
First Printing: February 1989
10 9 8 7 6 5 4 3 2 1

Library of Congress Cataloging-in-Publication Data

Sher, Barbara.
  Teamworks! : building support groups that
guarantee success.

  1. Small groups.   2. Self-help groups.   3. Group
relations training.   I. Gottlieb, Annie.   II. Title.
HM133.S515   1989   302.3′4   88-40097
ISBN 0-446-51461-6

Designed by Giorgetta Bell McRee

●●● Acknowledgments

I am pleased to thank a lot of people for this book. First, my parents, Sam and Nettie Sher, who in my childhood listened to me with curiosity and interest whenever I would hold forth on some new idea. I also thank them for the years I watched them make Thanksgiving and Christmas dinners for the pensioners who came into The Torch Club in East Los Angeles, our family bar. I saw them day after day help old people or Spanish-speaking people fill out complicated forms, deal with bureaucracies, and battle impersonal authority. I'd like to give credit to the other customers of The Torch Club, working men and women who let me act like a big shot behind the bar when I was still wet behind the ears, and who slipped me money when they heard I was going off to college. I'd like to thank the barmaids who showed me what it was like to be tough and kind at the same time.

I'd also like to thank my big brother Arthur, who taught me how to read and how to be brave, and my baby brother Kenny, who loved and admired me without reservation whether I deserved it or not. I'd like to thank my sons, Danny and Matthew, who always kept me company, praised and encouraged me, and never said no when I asked for any kind of help—from their opinions on my writing to licking stamps and sealing envelopes. I also thank them for showing me how brothers (and sisters, for they have one) really like to look out for each other, and for letting me know that my encouragement helped them dare the adventures they undertook.

When I track back my belief that people should respect and help each other, and in the notion that I might ever have something worth saying, this is always where it takes me.

I want to give credit to my teachers: Dan Casriel, who taught me the strength and healing power of peer groups; Bill Gordon of Synectics, who taught me to treat half-baked ideas with respect and thereby turn them into great ones; and Richard Bolles, who always took an interest, and encouraged and advised me from the beginning of my Success Team enterprise.

And thanks to those you might call my students (the people you'll be reading about here) and many others who worked tirelessly to share their belief in the principles of *Wishcraft* and *Teamworks!*, by running workshops or bringing me to their towns to run them, and who taught me at least as much about resourcefulness and ingenuity as I taught them.

My deepest thanks to you all.

Barbara Sher

Heartfelt thanks to Jacques Sandulescu, Clyde Taylor, Joann Davis, and to all the Success Team veterans who so generously contributed their experiences to this book.

Annie Gottlieb

Contents

● ● ●
Introduction

This book is designed to get you all the support you need to make you a winner.

You're about to learn how to create a variety of Success Teams, teams of all sizes and shapes, teams that will cheer you up, cheer you on, help you out, keep you going, and refuse to let you lose. You're also about to hear what happened to a lot of people who put together such teams for themselves and made some wonderful dreams come true.

I think you're going to have a lot of fun reading *Teamworks!* If you're anything like me you love to hear stories of ordinary people with no special "winning attitudes" who succeeded in achieving cherished goals. And if you're like me, you'd like to know what steps got them there. *Teamworks!* is full of those stories, stories of people who discovered something that was lying right in plain sight and put it into action. That something is support. I'm proud to say that I helped show many of them how to do it.

But I had to learn it for myself first, because like most other Americans, I was raised to believe you're supposed to make it on your own. As a child I could see that people were unique and had very different types of potential. But even then I had a strong sense that many of them, maybe even people I loved, maybe even me, were not going to fulfill that potential. In Detroit, where I'm from, a factory town full of new immigrants from Europe and the South all struggling to make it, I saw people trying to teach their kids to be tough so they'd survive. I didn't see them encouraging each other to try for cherished goals. And I had no idea what anyone was supposed to do about it.

I grew up to do a lot of struggling myself, raising a family on my own and working to get food on the table. But I happily fell into some work I was good at and wound up being trained and hired as a group therapist. I was a group therapist for many years before I understood that one of the reasons people were willing to take big chances and make such amazing emotional progress was that they were being encouraged by a roomful of friends who really cared about them, who wanted to see them succeed. Watching the exchanges of support among us made me want to try that same thing on goals that weren't therapy. I began to design a similar system for people who were trying to attain dreams such as sailing around the world or becoming a physicist, getting a decent apartment or learning to sing. And I came up with the Success Team.

A Success Team is a small group of people whose only goal is to help every member of the team get what he or she wants. Sounds simple. But no one I knew had such a team, including me. The first thing I did was put together a Success Team for myself. And it worked! I, who am not noted for my self-discipline or persistence, or for doing anything I don't have to do (see chapter one), found myself moving step-by-step toward some rather ambitious goals. And the other members of my team were doing exactly the same thing. I began to realize I was on to something big.

With the help (and goading) of my team, I put together some seminars and taught people how to find what they wanted, how to make a plan, and how to work in Success Teams. The results were phenomenal. People who had never even attempted to create the lives they wanted were now getting them. The media heard of it and started writing about the teams. I was invited to explain what was happening on television and radio shows, and I began to travel all over the country running seminars and putting people into Success Teams. In a short time there were too many people for me to handle alone, so I wrote *Wishcraft* and sent it out in my place.

TEAMWORKS!

1...

The Team Difference

GOING IT ALONE . . .

Sally is a forty-six-year-old history teacher in a small Pennsylvania town. She likes her job, she likes her life, but deep inside she has a dream. Since she knows it's just a dream, she's never really even put it into words. It's just a picture: a little house in a sunny place, by bright blue water, and inside the house, at a square white table, Sally, writing.

That is the picture in the center of Sally's heart. And the chances are that's where it's going to stay. Because in broad daylight, Sally is embarrassed that she ever dared to imagine herself a writer. And everybody knows that people on teachers' salaries don't get to have houses by the sea. Sally figures that's why dreams are called "dreams." They're nice—and then you wake up to reality.

Kelley graduated from Columbia University with a degree in English literature over ten years ago. Since then he's gone from job to job, and is now an editor in a technical publishing house. Kelley was reasonably satisfied with his life—or maybe the word is "resigned"—until he fell in love with Penny, a copy editor he met through his job. Their marriage revived his vision of the life he'd really love to live. Kelley's dream is to go to

1

chiropractic school and then live and practice in a small town. Penny would love that, because she could get her hands into the earth, study ornamental horticulture, and start her own landscaping business. Unfortunately, neither of them can see how any of this is ever going to happen. Chiropractic school takes four years and is expensive. Neither Kelley nor Penny has much money saved, and they have no idea how they can leave their jobs, live, and finance such an ambitious move.

Anita and Helen are lawyers working for a large utility company. They never imagined when they were in law school that they'd wind up pushing paper in an office, just like secretaries—and not getting paid much more. They're discouraged and disillusioned, but they both have too much invested in their law degrees to change careers. So they go out to lunch together and commiserate, hoping that they'll learn to live with their situations—or maybe win the lottery.

Philip is a bright high school student in a large city high school. He's in his junior year and has been advised to start applying to colleges, take some honors classes, and really buckle down for good grades. He knows he should be doing all these things, and he knows he's going to hate himself if he doesn't. But he keeps evading his school advisor, and he blows up at his parents every time they ask him what he's doing about college. The truth is, Philip isn't sure he'll be able to carry off all those honors classes and make a good showing. And there's something about writing that college application essay, the one about how great he is and why they should let him in, that he simply cannot tackle. These feelings are so unpleasant that he's courting ideas of becoming a truck driver or a rock drummer. He spends his time watching music videos and trying to forget the whole thing.

Jackie just got fired from a Fortune 500 company. Now she's supposed to be out looking for another job. But the job she had, which was too political and high-pressure for her, wore her down so badly in the last year that she has no stamina for an interview. She's sure she'll never be able to fake the bright, capable attitude she needs. And anyway, she's lost her self-

We all love to read in magazines about how successful people made it to the top. I look forward to the day those successful people will be quoted as saying, "I got there with a little help from my friends."

That's how I made it, and I hope *Teamworks!* will help you make it in the same way.

cently we spontaneously formed a *Wishcraft* working group of six dynamic people who get together one evening a week."

I heard that classified ads for "*Wishcraft* working groups" appeared in newspapers from Albuquerque to Long Island, that college instructors were using *Wishcraft* as a text in classrooms, and companies were using it to create crackerjack work units. Commuter colleges started running teams on their computer networks! It was astounding. I couldn't wait to open the mail every day.

But in the mail there was also another kind of letter: "How do I find a team when I'm in a town where I don't know anyone?" "My dream is to do what you do. I want to make my living helping people reach their goals. How can I get started?" "Do you have any materials I can use to teach these techniques to others?" "I love your book, but can you send me more information about Success Teams?"

Teamworks! is the answer to all those letters. In it are instructions for creating everything I designed, and the many colorful and ingenious variations designed by dozens of other people who wrote me, as well as stories of successful teams from all over the world. *Teamworks!* is the other half of *Wishcraft*. If there is anything dear to your heart that you would love to make happen, having a team behind you can make your chances better remarkably good.

The time has clearly come for the systematic creation of many kinds of support groups; their value is being seen by all of us in every endeavor. Hundreds of people have been creating their versions quietly in their own corners for years. It's my good luck that so many of them have found *Wishcraft* to be useful and have contacted me. Without expecting it I've become part of a Network of Networks, a Success Team made up of Success Teams, a world that has been building itself, as many of our visionary authors have exhorted us to do since I was in college in the 1950s.

I invite you to take the ideas in *Teamworks!* and adapt them in any way that works for you. There's nothing mystical or difficult about the team-building techniques in this book. They are simply ways of focusing our natural capacity for helpfulness and resourcefulness so that it can carry us to our individual goals.

Wishcraft: How To Get What You Really Want was written to teach people how to find out what they wanted, and how to make a realistic, practical plan for getting it, and in it I put a few brief instructions for creating Buddy Systems.

I continued to teach people how to create and run Success Teams in my seminars. (I'll show you how to run those seminars, too.) And in the seminars I found I was designing new kinds of support groupings all the time. The basic idea—a team whose only goal is to help its members attain their goals—seemed able to stretch and change itself into many shapes. I'd put participants into pairs (Buddy Systems) and have them help each other formulate their dreams and define the obstacles in achieving them. Then I'd combine two or three pairs into a planning group (Success Team) where they'd help each other design detailed plans, share resources, and offer each other any assistance they could. I'd invite friends and other guests to come to the seminar to offer their ideas (Brainstormings) and share their knowledge and give advice and help (Barnraisings). If the room had too many people in it for that to work properly, I'd make everyone run around with a pad and pencil, spending two minutes each telling their goals, their obstacles, and asking for suggestions from as many people in the room as possible (The Networking Game). The variations seemed endless! "This is a picnic!" I once said to a woman who was watching all the action. "It looks more like a madhouse," she laughed. "No," I said, "I know what it is. It's like a hundred birthday parties all at once, and everyone is getting presents." And I felt childishly happy, as if the whole thing was really my birthday party.

In the midst of all this, the mail from *Wishcraft* started rolling in. It was overwhelming. Clearly some nerve had been touched. I wasn't the only one in the country who wanted to find some practical, humane way to success.

"We've read *Wishcraft* and started our own Success Team, and wait until you hear what we've all done! We've used your idea to create a support network in Europe for American opera singers looking for jobs," said a letter from Germany. "In order to surround myself with a really competent support group I've bought and given away twenty-one *Wishcrafts* and have ordered seven more!" A man from Los Gatos, California wrote, "Re-

confidence, and doubts her ability to do good work anymore. She'd just give up and get a routine job . . . but she graduated with top honors from one of the most prestigious business schools in the country! She really loved big business, and she still does. She just doesn't think it loves *her* anymore.

Ellen lives on the military base in the Middle East with her husband and two teenage children. She's feeling very cut off and isolated, even though the other military wives on the base are very friendly. They feel cut off, too, and Ellen and her friends often talk wistfully about how exciting everything seems back in the States, according to the magazines they're reading. They wish they had the opportunity to start small businesses, or to get their bored children into interesting activities like theater or computers. They feel that because they're all so much alike, so stuck in the same situation, and so out of touch with the variety of opportunities available in an American city, they don't have much of a chance.

Quinn is a very good tennis player. He lives in a small town in Idaho and works at a golf and tennis club as an assistant. More than anything, he wants to get good enough to play on a well-known international team in Europe. He's very close to the grade he needs, but he doesn't know how to improve his game just that little bit more, or how to contact the team and get a chance to try out for it. Quinn's family is disappointed in his choices—they wanted him to go into business—and they have a hard time encouraging him. So he's very much on his own, and he feels stuck.

Roz is in her late fifties. She's spent twenty-five years taking care of her family, and the last five taking care of a sick husband. When she was a child, she was a successful actress, and she still misses that atmosphere, the fun and creativity and excitement of show business. But she figures there's no point in thinking about it at this late date. She got what life handed her, and she'll try her best to settle for that.

These are stories about the way we usually do things—which, as often as not, means we *don't* do them. Oh, we do a lot.

Don't get me wrong. We get to work in the morning, we get the bills paid, the diapers changed, breakfast on the table, the report written, the papers graded—all that hard stuff we have to do. But often we don't do precisely the things we most *want* to do, because they don't seem that important; or because we think they're impossible; or because we don't know how to do them; or because the risk and effort feel too great; or because nobody else cares if we do them or not. Then we languish in lives and jobs that don't quite fit, and we think that's just the way life is—even though something inside us keeps protesting that there must be more.

Years ago, when I was working as a group therapist and raising two kids alone, I was not happy with my life. There were so many things I had wanted to do and be. One day I had a brainstorm. I thought, "I'm so clever at running groups. I could run these on the *Queen Elizabeth 2* and get free trips to Europe, visit Oxford and Cambridge, and maybe even find a wonderful husband." So I ran upstairs and wrote all this down. I was on fire. Mind you, this had happened fifty times before, but I always forget that when I get inspired. I immediately got on the phone, called directory assistance, and asked for the number of the *QE2*. I actually got as far as calling the *QE2* offices. They said, "I'm sorry, you have to call London. Who are you, anyway?" At least I *thought* they said that. That's what I heard . . . so I hung up and threw away the piece of paper. That was the end of *that* plan—one of my ninety-eight great plans for fame, fortune, glory, and being admired for what I do best. It was about the ninety-fourth that didn't work.

I kept trying to remember to stop myself, and to just raise my children, to try to find the electric bill and pay it before they turned out the lights. I kept telling myself, "Look, you are mediocre. You are not special. Einstein is special. Barbra Streisand is special. You're not special. It's a neurotic thing to do that. Don't do that!" So I would walk around *not doing that*! I'd keep the kitchen clean for about two and a half days running, and then I'd get this urge to go on Broadway . . .

That urge—to do more, *be* more, make real the vision in your mind's eye—is basic to human beings. And it has to be honored. Deep down, we all know that. That's why our dreams never die, even after years of neglect. As hard as I tried, I could never completely convince myself that survival and security are all that life is about. My instincts were right. They're not.

Principle 1: If you have a dream in your heart, you'd better take it seriously. That dream is a clue to who you really are and who you can become.

You've heard that before, haven't you? Hundreds of books and thousands of magazine articles start out by saying, "You *can* have it all!" and then proceed to tell you how. Their advice varies, but it usually boils down to two points:

1. First and most important, you've got to believe. This used to be called "the Power of Positive Thinking." In this new age it is called "You create your own reality," but it's the same thing.

2. You've got to develop self-discipline. Under this heading come various techniques for learning persistence and overcoming procrastination.

In other words, all you have to do is get your mind right, get your act together, and the world is yours.

Unfortunately, that is easier said than done. I know. I tried.

I have visualized, and I have affirmed, and I have ested, and I have primaled, and I have breathed, and I have played motivation tapes in my sleep, and I have looked in the mirror and loved my face. Once I even told myself I deserved success. I believed it, too—for about two days. And two days only. There was no way to make any of it last any longer. I clearly didn't have the required character. If loving myself and beaming forth positive energy was beyond me, forget about self-discipline and getting organized. Given a choice between starting an exciting new project and watching *Casablanca* on TV, I'll take Bogie any day. I'll even take *All My Children*. I tried all that good advice. And all that happened was that the years drifted by, I smoked, I stopped, my weight went up, it went down, my children grew taller . . .

Principle 2: I have no right to tell you to take your dream seriously unless I'm sure I can show you how to get it—without becoming a better person first. Otherwise, I'm just inviting you to be disappointed.

The only reason I'm sure I can show you how to get it is because I got mine—and I'm no better than I ever was. I never will be. I've given up. And yet I have started two successful businesses, co-authored two books—one of them a bestseller—and toured the country several times, talking on radio, TV, and in front of groups, being applauded for what I do best. Now that that need has been fulfilled, I'm starting on a new, quieter dream. This eager, gregarious Leo who loved large audiences to admire her is metamorphosing into—a scholar! Not an academic. Just someone who loves to learn—all about Dante and history and the Hebrew Bible and the Middle Ages—and always did, but had other things to do first. That's what happens after success. You come to another, deeper layer of yourself. (My next book will be about that.)

But how did someone like me get successful in the first place?

What finally made the difference in my life was not some magical formula or spiritual conversion. It was so down-to-earth you won't believe it. I decided to go for what I wanted whether I deserved it or not, and if I couldn't get it by myself, like a good American should, well, I wasn't proud—not anymore—I was going to get some help.

Mind you, I reached this point out of desperation. In this culture, asking for help is looked upon with about as much approval as going on welfare. If we're men we're supposed to be independent, and if we're women we're supposed to give help, not get it, and anyway, who'd want to help with our personal dreams when they're having enough trouble with their own? (It turns out that's exactly why they'd want to help, but we'll get to that in a minute.) Actually, if we took a closer look, we would see that everybody who ever succeeded and stayed human in the process had a lot of help: a wife, a husband, a secretary, a father-in-law, a mentor, an old boys' network. But our culture does not acknowledge this fact. Our hero is called the *Lone* Ranger even though he has Tonto at his side at all times.

So by acknowledging that I couldn't make it on my own, I thought I was admitting defeat. I'm a hopeless case? All right, I know a few other hopeless cases. We've got nothing to lose. We might as well lean on each other. I called a few friends who I knew had been struggling along the same way and got them all together in my living room. I said, "Look. I'll make a deal with you. I'll help you do what you want to do if you will *make* me do what *I* want to do. I don't want you to leave it up to me to do what I want to do, because I won't do it!" So we started meeting every week. We gave each other inspiration, practical help, and support. I had ideas for them when they ran dry. They had guts for me when mine failed. And by God, it worked.

Principle 3: People have better ideas for each other than they have for themselves.

Principle 4: People have more courage for each other than they have for themselves.

It's not important for the purpose of this book why these two principles are true. They just are. You know it, too, if you've ever tried to cheer up a discouraged friend and found yourself getting enthusiastic about her project, buzzing with ideas, really wanting it to work. All the imagination, hope, and boldness that are so often blocked when it comes to your own dreams —because you're vulnerable there, or afraid—come rushing out when you're thinking for a friend. And they flow out of your friends whenever they think for you. The combination of affection and problem-solving is a heady one. It makes the helper feel like a true friend, or sister or brother—valuable, wise, and encouraging. And it makes the person being helped feel respected and safe. In this new kind of team I'd invented, everybody got to play both roles. It was really a kind of ideal family—the kind all of us had always wanted but could never find.

They were tough and loving, my first team. They wouldn't

let me get away with a thing. One of my wishes was to design a seminar to show people how they could start their own support teams. In the middle of working on it I had to go to the hospital to have an operation. The next day my team came in to see me and said, "How do you feel?"

I croaked, "Fine . . ."

They said, "How are your hands?"

I said, "My hands? They didn't operate on my hands."

They said, "Great!", gave me a pencil and a piece of paper, pushed the table up, and said, "Write!" I started to laugh, which was dangerous—it nearly killed me—but I got that seminar written.

One evening, when we were sitting around in a cozy circle, laughing, writing, swapping ideas and questions and phone numbers and disaster stories and success stories, I got suspicious. I thought to myself, "Wait a minute. This is too easy. This is cheating. Getting what you want is supposed to take struggle, sacrifice, and pain."

Then another little voice in my head answered, "Is it? Or could it be that the reason this feels so good is because it's the way human beings are really supposed to do things?"

I remembered reading something about how the early settlers in this country got their barns built. I looked it up. This is what I found out. When farmers had a barn to build, did they try to do it singlehanded and then blame themselves for failing? Of course not. They invited all their neighbors over for a working party—a barn-raising. They called a team. And it was a team that worked on the principle of "I'll help you raise your barn (or quilt your quilt, or shuck your corn) because I know you'll help me raise (quilt, shuck) mine."

When it come to "raising" those elaborate structures of ideas, plans, and actions that are our personal goals, we modern people have not been so smart. We keep trying to do it alone. We blame ourselves for failing. And then we try even harder to make ourselves stronger, braver, thinner, more self-disciplined, more self-loving, more Positive, more organized. It's as foolish and self-defeating as deciding to pump iron until you can build your barn alone.

I had spent years trying to turn myself into a spiritual Arnold Schwarzenegger in order to do something I should never have considered doing by myself. All those years I thought I needed a character transplant, when what I really needed was a team. I needed buddies, I needed mentors, I needed loyal defenders—people to run interference for me when I couldn't do it for myself. I needed clear heads to think for me when mine was cloudy with discouragement and doubt. I needed somebody to hold my hand when I was caving in. I needed somebody to drive me across town. I needed somebody to steer me toward the right information. I needed somebody who would teach me skills, who'd sit down and get me ready to talk to whoever I had to talk to. I needed someone who believed in my dreams. I needed real help. And so do you. Everybody does (at least everybody I'd want to have coffee with). That's because we are placental mammals. We did not come out of eggs, like snakes. We started out inside another human, and we're built to interact with other humans. That's how we function best.

Discovering this fact transformed my life, and it has transformed the lives of thousands of people who have used the *Teamworks!* principles in a variety of forms, from the most informal—When you have a problem to solve, ask everyone you know!—to the most structured—a team that holds weekly business meetings for personal goals. Nine of the people whose teams have changed their lives are the nine dreamers and underachievers whose sad stories I told you at the beginning of this chapter. Good news: that's not how it really happened. *This* is what happened.

. . . AND WITH A TEAM

Sally is a forty-six-year-old history teacher in a small Pennsylvania town. She likes her job, she likes her life, but she has a dream in her heart that just won't quit, and one day she decides not to keep it to herself any longer. Instead, she'll share it with a group of people and see if they have ideas for her. Sally decides to throw an idea party.

She considers having an intimate brainstorming brunch with her three best women friends. That's one way to do it. But since she wants all the bright ideas she can get her hands on, she decides to pull in a larger group: her school's PTA, of which she is a board member. Every parent, teacher, and student gets an invitation:

I HAVE A DREAM. DO YOU?
LET'S HELP EACH OTHER MAKE THEM COME TRUE.

••• IDEA PARTY •••

BRING YOUR DREAM,
YOUR BRAIN,
AND SOMETHING TO EAT.

CAMBRIA H.S. AUDITORIUM

MARCH 8, 1989

7:00 P.M.

Forty-seven people show up. If each one of them got up in front of the room, confided a dream or goal to the group, and asked for ideas, they'd be there all night. But Sally has come prepared for this. She hands out a pack of 3 × 5 file cards, pencils, and small pads of paper. On a card, each person is to write his or her name, fondest dream ("What do you want?"), and the biggest obstacle to getting it ("What's the problem?"). Sally's card says, "Sally K. Dream: small house by the sea in a warm climate, where I could write. Problem: lack of money." With her card pinned to her blouse, and pencil and paper in hand, she plunges into the fertile chaos of the Networking Game. She tells the audience how to proceed, says "Begin!", and goes down to join them.

All around the room, people are running breathlessly up to each other, blurting out their dreams and problems, and scribbling down all the ideas, leads, names, and phone numbers the other person can come up with in one minute, before the timekeeper yells "Switch!" Somebody laughs wildly, shouts "Eureka!" and starts waving her hand. Pencils fly, voices roar, and the room crackles with energy as obstacles fall before the force of concerted brainpower. It's the first time Sally has ever dared to say her dream out loud, and here she is saying it over and over.

After playing "the game" for about half an hour, she has written down these ideas for getting a house by the sea without much money:

—advertise in newpapers in coastal areas, offering services as house-sitter
—write great short story—apply for scholarship at seaside writers' colony
—check out new resorts, suggest they run writers' work-shop for publicity
—check out house-swap ads in travel mags
—ditto in Foreign Service newsletter
—drive along coast, look for house you like, knock—say, "I'm a writer, could you rent me a room?"
—join forces with other would-be writers, rent big house together
—see Joe J. after—has friend w/house Gulf Coast FL— empty most of year

Sally thinks some of these ideas are better than others, but her dream no longer looks quite so impossible. She will leave the auditorium tonight with at least two or three ideas that could actually get her that house by the sea for part of each year. If she's a self-motivated person, Sally can pursue these ideas on her own. But she doesn't have to. If the idea of knocking on a stranger's door makes her palms clammy, if she knows that list of ideas is going to wind up on the back side of a grocery list, she has another option: she can ask the group if anyone would like to be part of an ongoing Success Team—four to six people who will meet to exchange help and ideas every week.

At each team meeting, Sally's teammates will ask her what concrete steps she's taken toward getting that house by the sea, and what steps she plans to take next week. They'll ask her if she needs a morale-boosting phone call, or someone to go with her to an interview. Whenever she's stumped, they'll give her ideas on how to take the next step: where to find out about writers' workshops, what to read, who to call. More than that, they'll help her with the really hard part of her dream. Because they think Sally needs to be writing even before she gets the house by the sea. In fact, they think she should be writing right now. So they'll start by making her bring in one page. Just one page. They'll even assign her the topic—a fantasy description of the house by the sea, maybe, or something autobiographical.

A big team called a group brainstorming has shown Sally that her dream is not impossible, and given her a dozen ideas for doing it. A small team called a Success Team lightens the burden of risk and effort by keeping track of her and helping her break down an intimidating goal into small, real steps. Most of all, teams make sure she'll do it because someone else cares that she does it.

Why are her teammates willing to do all these things for Sally?

Simple. Because she's doing the same for them.

Kelley and Penny came to see me as a kind of last resort. Their dream of living and working in a small town just wouldn't go away. They'd heard from a friend that I believed—and had proved—that no dream is impossible . . . and that every deeply cherished dream is a necessity. That was what Kelley and Penny wanted to hear, but they still doubted that the financial obstacles to their dream could be overcome. I matched them up with four other people who were waiting to start a weekly Success Team.

The team put their heads together, and they came up with a daring plan that Kelley and Penny would never have dreamed of on their own. One teammate knew an absentee farmer in upstate New York who was looking for a caretaker to live on his country property. Penny could move up to the farm, rent-free, and earn money doing freelance copyediting for the state university. Meanwhile, she'd start growing a garden, learning landscaping, and making friends and connections in the nearby town. With the team's urging, Kelley sent for information about chiropractic schools, and found one on Long Island that would let him work for the school to help with tuition. He also took out loans. He and Penny would visit each other as often as possible, and Kelley could feel that he'd already begun to put down roots in his beloved small town.

It wasn't easy. After two years they really hated being apart, and Kelley was often tired from his grueling class schedule. Penny had kept in touch with her teammates, and she invited them up to the farm for a morale booster. The five of them put

• • • *13*

together a wonderful scheme to cheer Kelley up. Penny appeared at his school and escorted him out to a limousine, owned and driven by a teammate's friend. She drove him upstate to the farm, served him a candlelight dinner, and said, "Happy birthday. Your present is under your plate." He looked and found the key to a car. Outside was a good little used car her teammates had helped her find for him.

No more bus rides! Kelley was so delighted that it put him back on track. He wanted to do something equally nice for Penny, so he called the team. "What does she want," he asked, "that I can get her with no money?"

"She wants you to be a great dancer," they told him.

On her birthday he brought her down to his school, a converted mansion from the turn of the century. His classmates (he'd used the team principle to bring them in on his plot) cleared the main hall for her arrival. When Penny showed up, Kelley was dressed in a borrowed tuxedo. He led her in and up to the first landing, a balcony overlooking the main hall. Music mysteriously started, and he took her in his arms and danced gracefully around the floor with her. He'd been taking lessons for five months, compliments of a fellow student who had once been a dance instructor!

The second two years passed much more easily than the first. Today Kelley is a successful chiropractor in the small town they both love. Penny is doing well with her own business, designing landscapes for homes in the area. She has a small staff and is very happy with her work. Living rent-free on the farm enabled them to pay off Kelley's loans quickly and save money, and they recently made the down payment on their own home. "The team showed us how we could work at what we loved, and take good care of each other at the same time," says Kelley. "It was the best thing that ever happened to us."

Anita, the utility-company lawyer, saw an ad in her local bookstore for people wanting to be in a Success Team. The next day she mentioned it to Helen, her friend and companion in the doldrums. They decided that they had nothing to lose—they'd join the team together.

After hearing their stories, their teammates asked, "Have the two of you ever considered opening your own law practice?"

Helen and Anita looked at each other, and they both admitted that they'd had that fantasy, but they'd never even mentioned it to each other, because it seemed so farfetched. "Why?" asked June, the secretary who was ultimately to become a city planner. "My brother's a junior partner in a new law firm in San Francisco. We'll ask him how the partners got started."

Today, two years later, Anita and Helen have their own law firm and their own clientele. "We're working twice as many hours, earning three times as much money, and having a hundred times as much fun," says Helen.

Philip's high school advisor heard about Success Teams and decided, in desperation, to try to start one. He called a group of students into his office, all of whom had been acting like Philip, avoiding the high-pressure problems of buckling down for good grades and getting their college essays written. He ran them through a series of *Teamworks!* team-building exercises and made them responsible for each other. Within the first week, they'd set up a study group that met three nights a week! In the advisor's office, they sat down in a circle and worked on each other's essays and applications, one by one, until every one of them was completed and sent off—before the deadline.

After Jackie was fired by her Fortune 500 company, her team thought she needed rest and rehabilitation before she started seriously looking for a new job. They tried to think of something that would make her feel better, but no vacation would do the trick. So they asked her, "When did you feel the best in your life?" It turned out that Jackie's happiest time had been her years in graduate school. The team convinced her to call up some of her old professors and see if there was a teaching assistantship available for a while—until she got her energy back. There was.

Jackie taught at her old graduate school for a semester and a summer session. By the end of that time, she had a completely new perspective. "Getting all that respect from the students, seeing how naive they were about the world out there, trying to prepare them—all that was just the medicine I needed," she says. "Now I can see that my problems at my company were not a reflection on me at all—or on the company. It was just a bad fit. I belong in a different kind of company. And guess what? If you want to find out what a company is really like before you apply for a job, work at a business school. The people there are so knowledgeable. I'm doing my research now, and doing it with care. I expect I'll be out there very soon, and I'll get a job that's right for me."

Ellen, the military wife living overseas, was sent my book *Wishcraft* by a relative in the States and read it with fascination. She realized that she and her friends could create the excitement they were missing right there on the army base. Ellen called together six other army wives to form a team. A number of their children wanted to be in the teams, too. They've just begun, but in the works are plans for starting their own theater production company (they've discovered quite a few people on the base who have experience in the theater); getting the base school to create an up-to-date computer club for interested kids—and two mothers who want to join it, too; and a possible mail-order, import-export business. Ellen herself wants to start a small publishing company and solicit personal stories from Americans living on military bases all over the world. She and her team are brainstorming about ways to promote the idea.

Quinn, the tennis player, got into a team through a *Teamworks!* seminar at the local junior college, and he started getting support for his dream right away. Now that he wasn't alone, he began to see what he'd just been too discouraged to realize before: that he had some opportunities very close to home. The tennis pro he most wanted to train with worked at the same club he did, and even knew who Quinn was. The pro was very busy, but with a lot of friendly prodding and encouragement from his teammates, Quinn composed a note to put on the man's desk and got up the nerve to talk to him.

Meanwhile, one of his teammates quizzed him about how to get in touch with the European team, and found out that Quinn knew the names of all the magazines that dealt with the world of tennis—a world his teammates were completely unfamiliar with. That didn't stop them from helping him. They had Quinn get copies of the tennis magazines, and they all sat around going through them until they found the person Quinn needed to contact. Then he went home, drafted a letter, and brought it back to the next meeting. Everyone liked it, and it got typed up and shipped off. Everything now awaits the answers to these letters, but Quinn says if he can't get time with the tennis pro at his club, he'll find another one, even if he has to move to a different part of the country. "I'm a grade 5, and I need to be a grade 6 to try out for that team," he said. "My path is clear now. I'm going for a 6."

Roz, the retired wife and mom who never got over her childhood love of show biz, was in a Success Teams workshop over eight years ago. I've kept up with her progress, and since she's been written up in *USA Today* and other places, you may have heard of her, too. The first thing she did with the help of her team was start her own taped radio show, *Rap and Rock with Grandma Roz*, which she got on the air in a middle-of-the-night spot. She was so popular that her station arranged to have her do celebrity interviews. Through her meetings with celebrities, she got a job working on location with a film company as a consultant. I'm waiting to hear what's next, but Roz is hard to get in touch with these days. She's too busy!

These people have all discovered "the team difference"—the difference between doing a lot less than you'd like and more than you ever dreamed possible. When you finish this book, you will know how to create Success Teams and other support systems for yourself, for the people you love, and for the clients you work with. You'll find out the best way to get to your peak performance—with friends and buddies cheering you on—the *Teamworks!* way.

2 ● ● ●

The *Teamworks!* Toolbox: How to Use This Book

Let's suppose you've got a dream—and a problem. A desire and an obstacle. Those are the two basic elements every human quest starts out with, like flint and sticks. The two questions I always ask at the beginning of my seminars are:

"What do you want?"
and
"What's the problem?"

As you start reading this book, I'd like you to think about something you want. Not something you want and are around the corner from getting—like wanting a house and having saved the down payment and being in the process of shopping. Not that kind of wish. Think of something close to your heart but far from your hands, something you've wanted for a while but don't really expect to get. Maybe you've already tried to get it and failed. Maybe you haven't tried for fear of failing. Or maybe you've never even thought of trying, because you're sure it's impossible. Whatever it is, you're pretty sure it would make you really happy if I could wave a magic wand and give it to you.

Your dream goal may be as precise as a $5,000-a-year raise, or as vague as a feeling that you ought to be working with people, not computer terminals. It may be the next step in your current career, or a complete leap into the unknown—like the utility company executive who longed to be a wildlife manager. It may be a lifelong wish to learn to paint, write, or play the cello, or a more recent wish to help out your community. It could be to get your apartment remodeled or to get married, to have a baby or lose the pounds you gained on the last one, to master a new sport or move to a new city.

Short of homicide or suicide—the ones where you can't change your mind—there are no right or wrong wishes. I've had people in my seminars apologize for wanting something "trivial" (to lose weight) or "materialistic" (a Porsche). Once a woman lawyer confessed that she wanted to be a *femme fatale*, and every feminist in the room flew to her feet, objecting. My response was that it's not my job, or anyone's on earth, to judge what you want. That's God's job. Want to marry a millionaire, or chuck it all and join the circus? Fine. My job is to show you how.

So what's the problem?

Answers will spring quickly to mind (like "Money!"). But if you'd like a fascinating glimpse into the problems behind the problems, you might try this exercise created by LaVaun Maier, a potter and writer in Milwaukie, Oregon, who leads classes in personal growth. LaVaun says she designed this exercise "to help people see how they keep themselves from knowing what they want."

—Take a large sheet of paper, 11" × 21" or bigger.

—With felt pens, draw yourself (stick figures are fine) in the lower left-hand corner of the page.

—In the upper right-hand corner, draw your "heart's desire," your goal; or, if you haven't identified it, simply represent an unspecified goal (using a bright heart, a radiant star, or a question mark).

—Now *quickly* sketch what keeps you from getting to your goal. Use symbols, colors, quick representations. Avoid words and analyzing.

—What do you see in the picture? What did you discover as you drew it?

"The results of these quick sketches are fascinating and never fail to surface unrecognized fears, faulty beliefs, or sabotaging behaviors [as well as real-world obstacles]," says LaVaun. "For example, one woman drew a stairway between herself and her goal. She drew herself falling down the stairs. She realized that—based on some previous experiences—she was afraid of 'falling on her face' if she should strive for some personal goal. She also saw that the lines for her steps were not connected; they looked insubstantial."

The images in this picture are familiar. I've heard a lot of answers to the question, "What's the problem?" And while the details vary, the basic things that keep most of us from getting what we want can be counted on the fingers of one hand. They are:

1) *Uncertainty*. Not knowing very clearly what we want.
2) *Money*. This includes both "I can't afford a Porsche" and "I can't quit this job even though I hate it, because I have to earn a living, feed my family, and keep up the mortgage payments."
3) *Time*. Includes both the lack of it ("I'm so busy earning a living and taking care of my kids that I don't have time to take piano lessons/go to night school/write a novel") and the inefficient use of it (disorganization, procrastination, etc.).
4) *Lack of information*. The woman whose "steps" were un-connected and insubstantial drew an expressive picture of this problem. You often start out ignorant of how to do anything you'd love to do but have never done be-fore. It's natural. But it's not bliss. When you don't know how to find a good music teacher or form a corporation, when you want to move to Sacramento or Sarasota but don't know anyone there, your dream can look like a sheer cliff face with no handholds or footholds.

And that brings us to:

5) *Negativity*, which includes fear ("What if I go in and ask for the raise and he says no?") and discouragement ("It won't work anyway, so what's the use?").

Negativity has a very interesting relationship to the first four problems on this list: it gives them more power. When you face the real difficulty of finding the right goal, or money, time, information, or skills, it's natural to feel discouraged and un-sure—especially if you've tried and gotten hurt before. But those feelings inhibit the hope, energy, and imagination with which you could have tackled the practical problems, and so the problems start to look larger. And the bigger they look, the smaller you feel, and the smaller you feel, the bigger they look . . . Besides, some seemingly practical problems are really negativity in disguise: "I don't have time to write," for instance, may really mean, "I'm scared to write." Finally, not getting what you want over a period of years also feeds negativity, so it's often the case that the more dissatified you are with your life, the less power you feel you have to change it.

That's why you need a team behind you. A *Teamworks!* type of team.

> *Teamworks! Team* (n.): A group of people, of any size, called together for the express purpose of helping you get what you want (and getting what they want in the process).

A team can be as small as one friend on the other end of the phone, or as large as an auditorium packed with 150 people or an open-ended national network. You need a team (we'll get to what kind of team in a minute) because it is the one kind of help that never fails to break the vicious cycle of negativity.

I know. As I already noted, I've tried positive thinking and affirmations and creative visualization and subliminal motiva-tion tapes. Used in isolation from other people and other tech-niques, all they do is lower my negativity, the way aspirin suppresses a fever. For a day or a week, I feel wonderful. I believe that anything is possible. Then I go out there unpre-pared, hit my first big real-world obstacle, and realize that I was wrong. Negativity is back with a vengeance. Having felt so good for one brief shining moment just makes me feel worse.

Teams combat negativity directly, too—much more power-fully than solitary techniques do—but they don't stop there. In a team, reviving hope is just the beginning. Teammates look at your dream with fresh eyes. They don't share your inner burden of fear and discouragement; in fact, they can have all the enthusiasm for your goals that they might not muster for their own. And because the team-building techniques you will learn in this book create a bond of the imagination and spirit, not an emotional entanglement, you'll see interest and acceptance in them that you hardly had yourself. Ten or twenty people believing in your goal can give you far more hope and courage than saying a mantra ten times before you go to sleep. But courage is not enough. You also need help—hard, practical help with problems 1 through 4.

If I were to send you straight into the lions' cage full of belief and hope and courage, I'd be guilty of murder. What I've got to do is get you a lion tamer's autobiography, a ticket to the circus, and an introduction to the lion tamer. He'd teach you how to hold the whip and chair while he runs at you with a big teddy bear, and then put you in with some really sleepy lions . . . and in a little while you'd be ready for your debut.

That is what a team does for you.

Because they have no negativity about your dreams, teammates look at your problems with unfettered imagination. They can brainstorm to help you clarify or set a personally tailored goal if you don't have one (problem 1). They can help you figure out how to get your dream for the least possible money—and then, how to get your hands on that sum (problem 2). They can help you schedule time to fit in those writing sessions, mile jogs, or promotional projects—and hold you to it with a strategically timed phone call ("Hi! It's Barbara. Got your running shoes on?") (problem 3). They can give you the phone number of their friend's uncle in Sacramento, the name of someone who knows all the singing teachers in town, the title of a book on starting your own small business, or a practice session for a job interview (problem 4).

Whenever you run into a fresh problem in the field, your team will brainstorm it with you. And when you are feeling down—because of rough weather in your life, or just because it's Monday—they'll make you put up an umbrella and keep going, step by step (problem 5). No team can promise that you'll never have a down day again. If you were in a good mood all the time, you wouldn't be human. With a team behind you, you'll still have negativity, but it will lose its power to stop you from getting what you want. And that means you'll have less of it, and take it a lot less seriously.

What kind of team do you need? A large one or a small one? Informal or highly structured? A team that meets once only, or once a month, or once a week? A team of people from all walks of life, or a team of colleagues from your field? All men, all women, or mixed? Friends or strangers? Fast-trackers or pleasure seekers? It depends on you: the kind of person you are, where you are on your life's journey, and what the main problems are that come between you and your goals.

A team is a tool. There are different kinds of teams, just as there are different kinds of tools for different tasks. The "toolbox" of this book is divided into three sections. I've called the first two sections Help Level 1 and Help Level 2, and the third, Variations on a Team.

Help Level 1 presents the more informal, unstructured, and occasional kinds of teamwork: phone and mail networks, computer networks, group brainstormings, monthly networking meetings, the Networking Game. You can create some of these teams at home, by yourself, with the minimum operating equipment—your phone, address book, and stamps. Some of them call for inviting over a small group of friends. The section concludes with ways of working with larger groups, such as your church, temple, Y, Junior League, PTA, or alumni association. All of these *Teamworks!* groupings are for getting ideas, rather than ongoing support. They can supplement the more intensive support systems in Help Level 2, or they can be used independently by people who need only inspiration, information, and contacts—those priceless resources offered by other people. Help Level 1 shows you how to locate and activate those resources so that you can draw on them whenever you need to.

You Will Want to Use Help Level 1 (pp. 27–70) if:
—most of your answers to the question, "What's the problem?" fit under problems 2 through 4 (money, time, and lack of information); or:
—what you want most is lots of good ideas; or:
—you are a self-starter once you get excited about a project (I know there are a few of you out there!); or:

—you are the kind of person who works best in informal or unstructured situations; or:

—you are something of a loner and don't enjoy groups, or can't meet because of distance or previous commitments; or:

—you belong to a large group or organization, and would like to galvanize it into a resource pool for yourself and every member; or:

—you're not ready to sign up for a team until you know more, and want to start by just sticking a toe in the water; or:

—you are working in a Success Team or buddy system (Help Level 2) and want to draw on a bigger pool of ideas and contacts; or:

—you are a natural-born networker and resource person who would like to start your own resource bank (see p. 43); or:

—you are, or would like to be, a professional working with people, helping them define and reach their goals (if so, look for the special professionals' guide further on in this "toolbox").

Help Level 2 presents a more intensive, intimate, and structured kind of teamwork: the Success Team of four or five people that meets weekly or every other week. Almost anyone can benefit from being in a Success Team—and get a kick out of it, too—but it is especially helpful to people who are in a challenging life transition, or who have problems with persistence. (Does that leave anyone out? I don't think so.)

You Will Want to Use Help Level 2 (pp. 71–177) if:

—you have a weight problem, or you've quit smoking three times, or you've jogged once; or:

—you feel you lack persistence, self-discipline, and character (like me); or:

—you are much better at doing what you have to do (because somebody else depends on it) than what you want to do (when only you depend on it); or:

—you tend to procrastinate and/or get things done at the last minute; or:

—your more practical problems (1 through 4) seem overwhelming; Or:

—fear and discouragement (problem 5) have played a large
part in your not getting what you want; or:

—you are (or want to be) a freelance worker, small-business
owner, or entrepreneur—someone who sets his/her own
objectives and deadlines and often works alone; or:

—you are a student trying to decide what you want to do
with your life; or:

—you want to make a major career change—a risky leap
into the unknown; or:

—you are a mother of grown children and you're re-
entering the work force; or:

—you are retired, and getting bored with golf, card games,
and TV; or:

—you have recently been laid off; or:

—you are, or want to be, a professional working in career-
change counseling, outplacement, vocational rehabilitation, high school or college career counseling, services
to the elderly, or corporate human-resources development (see the Professionals' Guide, coming up).

The third section of this book, Variations on a Team, en-
courages you to get creative with the basic *Teamworks!* principles
and custom-design a team to fit your unique situation. For
inspiration, I'll show you six goal-oriented and six play-oriented
variations.

You'll want to use Variations (pp. 179–224) if:

—you'd rather work with one other person than with a
group (see The Buddy System, p. 182, for a two-person
mini-team); or:

—your husband, wife, or kids are your team—or if you
wish they were! (see The Home Team, p. 187); or:

—you'd like to join forces with a group of people who all
have the same goal—to lose weight, to find a mate, to
find a job (see The Job Club p. 192), The Create-an-Event
Team (p. 194), Kick-the-Habit Clubs (p. 198), Boy (Girl)

    Scouts of America (p. 211), and The White Elephant Sale
(p. 213); or:

—you're a pro (actor, writer, singer, golfer, entrepreneur,
racing car driver) who'd like to make some extra money,
or if you're just starting out and need guidance (see
Mentor/Apprentice Teams, p. 208); or:

—you work in a field where finding jobs, clients, or customers is a problem (such as acting, singing, dancing,
psychotherapy, carpentry, or crafts) (see Guilds, p. 201).

Then comes "dessert": salons and soirees, play-readings and
town meetings, Sunday brunch and Cafe Society—playteams
you can call on when you just feel like learning about something, from superconductivity to Italian opera, or when you
want a more interesting reason than cocktails to have people
over. I put in these social variations on a team (they're also
terrific variations on a party) because one of my dreams is to
restore the exchange of ideas and the art of conversation as
ways of enjoying old friends and making new ones.

    Help yourself to dessert if:

—you feel that your life is becoming all work and no play;
or:

—you're getting bored with spectator entertainment (i.e.
sitting in front of the VCR/TV); or:

—for you, the best part of seeing a movie or reading a
good book is talking about it afterward; or:

—you sometimes catch yourself wishing you could go back
to school, just to learn; or:

—there is a subject—artistic, scientific, political, philosophical—that you're very curious about; or:

—you love live concerts or plays but don't have the time
and/or money to go; or:

—you work, or play, in the arts and would like to share
your creations with others; or:

—you've moved to a new town, or been divorced or widowed, and need to meet new people.

PROFESSIONALS' GUIDE TO *TEAMWORKS!*

If you are a professional who works with people, or if you'd like to start your own business helping others get what they want and do what they love, you've come to the right place. The team techniques in this book will help you find more clients, serve them more powerfully—and protect yourself from burn-out, the number-one occupational hazard in your field. The whole book will give you ideas you can use, but in addition, instructions specifically tailored to you and the population you work with will be found on the following pages:

—If you are a corporate manager or HRD trainer-developer, see p. 158 for corporate dream teams
—If you are a high school or college career counselor, see p. 163
—If you are in outplacement, see p. 167
—If you are in vocational rehabilitation, or work with depressed populations such as displaced homemakers, recovering addicts, the homeless, or the chronically un-employed, see p. 167
—If you work with senior citizens in retirement commu-nities or nursing homes, see p. 174
—If you are an independent career developer, or if you want to start your own *Wishcraft/Teamworks!* counseling service, see p. 162. This is a package of services you can offer.

You're ready to use and enjoy *Teamworks!* Read the book, pick the team-building techniques you like, and then go out and get yourself some teammates. Experience the amazing dif-ference it makes to have a team behind you.

PART I
HELP LEVEL 1: BUILDING INFORMAL SUPPORT SYSTEMS

3...

One-on-One Support

You have a dream. And you have a problem—something (or things) that's keeping you from getting it.

The basic principle of *Teamworks!* is: Don't remain alone with that situation. To get out of it, let someone else in on it. And the simplest, most basic way to do that—the little building block with which all of *Teamworks!* begins—is:

TELL A FRIEND

—Pick up the phone and call the most imaginative person you know.

—Have lunch with your best friend and tell her/him.

—Tell your spouse, lover, child, or mother—*if* that person is also your best friend.

This is not quite as simple as it seems.

It's very different to tell someone a private dream than to just think it. Dreaming in private is very safe and pleasant. It requires no further action. It might even replace action. But if you're taking the chance of revealing a long-hidden wish, you're playing with real money, not Monopoly money. The experience can be powerful and unsettling, but it is always exciting. When I instruct people in my seminars to tell another person what they want, and then ask them how it made them feel, some common answers are "nervous," "guilty," "embarrassed," and "frustrated," or "excited," "frightened," "exhilarated," and sometimes "sad." Why so many reactions to such a simple action?

Because saying what you really want can be a little risky. There are things it's acceptable to want—like a promotion, or to get organized—and you can tell those with ease, but the closer a wish is to your heart, the tougher it can be to say. A real wish is vulnerable, to both embarrassment and hurt: embarrassment because you can almost hear someone laughing at its grandiosity, and hurt because you've been reminded of a longing that you think will never be met. Hurt because if you've ever gone out on a limb for a big wish before and gotten your heart broken, you may find that you're waking up some old feelings—and fears of getting hurt again.

That's why I'm saying that the first person you tell should usually be a friend. There's a technique for turning your family into your team later on in this book (see The Home Team, p. 187). But sometimes your family will greet the revelation of your dream with an indignation born of panic: "What about your future? What if something happens to you? What about us?" Most friends, by contrast, have nothing to fear from your confession. They can more easily listen with interest. That's just the response you need.

People in my seminars report that the act of telling another person what they want is freeing and releases great energy. Why? Because someone has listened to your impossible dream with real interest—and interest equals respect. That is, something that seemed farfetched or frivolous to you is being treated as though it were quite reasonable, even admirable. That can create a new feeling all by itself. We've all had the experience of being grilled by critics and scoffed at by skeptics. To have someone lean forward and listen with interest and enthusiasm when you tell them your dreams is not a daily occurrence for most of us. It starts something remarkable happening inside.

ONE-ON-ONE BRAINSTORMING

Sit down with a friend in a place where you're both comfortable and can be relatively undisturbed for an hour.

—If your friend also wants to solve a problem, divide the available time in half.

Have a pen and a pad of paper handy. Tell your friend what you want and what the problem is. Here's a way to phrase it that often stimulates more ideas in a brainstorming:

—How many ways can I get a house on the ocean when I have no money?

Both of you now come up with every solution you can think of as quickly as possible. You will find that you inspire each other.

—Don't try to pre-edit your list, or to have only "good" (sober, realistic, workable) ideas at this stage. You don't want to get self-conscious.
—Include dumb and crazy ideas too—one of them could be a clue to the best idea you'll get. Loosen up, in whatever way that's natural to you.
—Write down every idea either one of you comes up with, with no exceptions.

And then, the key to a first-rate brainstorming:

1. Carefully go over the ideas one by one, and find something useful in every idea on the resulting list.
2. Take the useless part and improve on it.

This is a surefire way to innovative solutions. Here's how it worked for one dreamer:

Sally, the schoolteacher who wanted to write in a house by the sea for little or no money, got several ideas from her brainstorming team. At first she thought some of the ideas (such as offering house-sitting services or renting a friend's cottage that stands empty most of the year) more promising than others. Going through her list a second time, using this technique, she found buried treasure in some of the less promising ideas:

—check out house-swap ads in travel mags
  Useful element: no money required
  Useless part: who'd want to come live in my apartment in a small Pennsylvania town?
  How to improve:
  —offer two months of northern summer to someone who hates heat
  —research local cultural resources, folk customs, natural wonders, etc. Make it attractive.
  —check out visiting faculty at local college

—write great short story—apply for scholarship at seaside writers' colony
  Useful element: it would get me writing and make me take myself seriously as a writer
  Useless part: it would take too long—and I'm not sure I'm good enough!
  How to improve:
  —get brochures from writers' colonies and see what their entrance requirements are
  —draw up an outline for a writing project
  —get together writing I've already done—from professional papers to private journal

That's how you turn an apparent dud of an idea into a source of inspiration.

You will almost always find that you and your brainstorming partner not only come up with ideas but also concrete suggestions and leads: someone to call for more information, an article in last week's magazine, the name of a local adult-education class or riding club.

Once even one friend knows about your dream and has given you ideas and suggestions, you have set a force in motion that will push you toward your goal. That force is called account-ability, otherwise known as good guilt. When you run into that friend again, she will want to know what happened: "How's it going? Did you find a house by the ocean?" If you have to say, "No, I didn't try," and your friend looks disappointed, you're going to feel worse for her than you do for yourself. That simple response of yours is all the accountability you need, and if you should go on to be in a Success Team—as described in Help Level 2—it is one of the major elements that will keep you moving until you reach your goal.

TIPS FOR BECOMING A PROFESSIONAL

One-on-one brainstorming is a valuable service that career de-velopers and *Wishcraft/Teamworks!* counselors can offer their clients.

If you're good at having ideas for other people, if you love nothing more than to give someone a creative suggestion and watch him run with it, you can do that for a living. All you need is imagination, resourcefulness and interest—and a way to find clients. (My suggestion for the last is to run a seminar, and in the next section, I'll tell you how.)

There are three interrelated one-on-one brainstorming ser-vices you can offer:

—Goalsearching: "What's your dream?"
—Troubleshooting: "What's the problem?"
—Resourcing: "Where can you find what you need?"

Goalsearching

When someone feels dissatisfied with what she is doing but doesn't quite know what she'd rather do, there's a technique to help her find precisely the right job or create a personally tailored goal that embodies what she loves in practical, do-able form.

First you need to:

—find out what she loves, and
—take the lead in imagining how that could be shaped into a real-world goal.

Two of the questions I like to use in goalsearch brainstorming are:

—"If I could wave a magic wand and give you anything you wanted, what would you ask for?"
—"What would you be doing in Paradise?"

When Andrea R., a twenty-six-year-old professional singer, came to see me, she was feeling discouraged by the competitive and product-oriented New York opera scene. "The idea is this perfect singer you're going to become, not an appreciation of the process of becoming a singer," she said. "And I felt that the audience was mostly people who like to spend a lot of money and other opera singers looking for flaws to pick on. I love to sing, but those weren't the people I wanted to sing for."

Andrea's answer to the magic wand question was, "I would have an audience of people who loved to hear, and I'd sing anything I wanted."

Here's what she'd be doing in Paradise:

singing
drawing
playing with children
teaching anything
helping people
being with my friends
organizing events
traveling (especially to unusual places)
petting animals
eating
dancing

wearing beautiful costumes and clothing
reading
writing letters to companies with my opinion about their
    advertising
being the center of attention
psychoanalyzing
taking baths
being by myself for a time every day
acting
going to movies and plays
having a good singing lesson

Andrea made her living working for an organization that provided services for the aged. I asked if she would like to travel
across the country performing for people in nursing homes.
She lit up at once, and I knew we had an idea we could work
with. Note how many items on her Paradise list are included
in this goal (singing, helping people, being with friends, organizing events, traveling, wearing beautiful costumes, being
the center of attention, acting). Andrea put the project together
(I'll give you details later) and has since performed with a partner, Nannette J., in nursing homes in Texas, Cape Cod, and
Florida, on their holiday weekends and vacations. They call
themselves "Lyrics a la Carte."

"We hand out flowers during our shows, when we sing 'Tra-
la, it's May' from *Camelot*," Andrea says. "People love that.
The show is all light stuff. We start with 'We Open in Venice'
from *Kiss Me Kate*, and we change the words for every place
we go: 'We open in Dallas, we next play Laredo,' or 'We open
in Falmouth, then on to Hyannis' . . . It's like music therapy.
You get people who are sitting there with no expression on
their faces, and you go in there and sing and their faces start
to light up. It happens all the time. We would get people just
crying and saying it brought back such memories. It really made
a difference, and that to me was very important."

That's the kind of goal to look for when you're doing goalsearch brainstorming. Try for the perfect solution first, even if
it seems impossible. The trouble with pursuing only the possible is that we actually have much less energy for it than for
a seemingly impossible but beloved goal. Andrea and Nannette

ran into all kinds of problems on the path to their nursing-home singing tour. "At every stage there was a major obstacle," says Andrea. "We had a horrible problem with our accompanist. Since we had very little money, we hired a student pianist, and the first show was a major disaster. She was playing in the wrong key. It was very embarrassing. And then she backed out before the next show, leaving us very little time to find another pianist. At the last minute we had to find someone who could sight-read very well. We finally solved that one by buying a big, fancy tape recorder with a donation from my stepmother, and making professionally recorded tape. And then there were the problems with the costumes . . ."

A great part of what kept Andrea and Nannette going, of course, was each other (see The Buddy System, p. 182). "I could never have done it alone," says Andrea. That's the kind of support this book is all about. But the other force that kept them going through all the problems and discouragements was their passion for what they were doing. Loving something is a surefire signal that you have a gift for it, or some aspect of it, and love is the energy which—coupled with support—will get you there.

The Look

When I'm trying to help clients find a goal, I watch for what I call The Look. I let them talk for a while. They might say, "Well, I'd like to be a nurse—you can always find a job—and there's a lot of money in real estate . . . but, oh, I'd love to sing . . ." or "I saw Montana last summer . . ." and suddenly their eyes change, and they look like they're falling in love. That's The Look. It means that you've hit paydirt. It most often comes when the person is talking about something she thinks will never happen. Yet out of all the things she could want in the world, that is the thing she will have the will to make happen—given sufficient encouragement and support. So watch for The Look when you use any of the following goalsearch questions with a friend or client.

Duluth, Minnesota, career counselor Melanie R. Keveles uses these questions, among others, to help find out what her clients love:

—"What do you do as naturally as breathing?"
—"What did you love to do as a child?"
—"Is there somebody doing something that you really admire?"

"My dream is for everybody on this planet to be doing what they love," says Melanie. "What I do is try to instill hope—get people thinking that maybe there's a possibility that they could do something they actually enjoy. What I do like breathing is brainstorm, so I try to be as creative as possible about it, and use these questions as catalysts for their thinking." Some of the ideas Melanie has come up with for her clients:

—for a woman working in a hospital, bored with her job, who loved music: set up a conservatory in the hospital—a room where patients and staff could come to practice and play ("Try starting from where people are, and then brainstorming beyond that.")
—for a former nurse who was trying to start a Color Me Beautiful business and wasn't getting it off the ground: contact the hospital flower shop or gift shop, and offer a Color Me Beautiful gift certificate as an alternative to flowers for new mothers and other patients.
—for a woman who, as a child, had loved to collect rare teddy bears and look for UFOs: "We figured out that the theme in there—her mission—is looking for rare things. She had never seen the significance of those things before. She began thinking about getting a job tracing lost items."
—for a former teacher forced to retire by a hearing problem: "As a result of working with one of the state agencies, she decided she wanted to do technical writing. But she wasn't getting any jobs, and there wasn't much energy behind her campaign. I started working with her and found that one of the things she really loves is food! I

asked her who she admired, and it turned out that there
was a woman in our community who writes a food column." The former teacher has now written six food
columns and sent them out to local newspapers all over
Wisconsin and Minnesota.

Melanie tells how a single suggestion can sometimes spark
a client's imagination and liberate her sense of possibility: "A
woman came in and said, 'I have to write a résumé and I don't
want to.' She had worked for a company that was going out
of business; she'd been there eighteen years. So I said to her,
'Let's forget about the résumé. What do you love to do?' She
said, 'What do you mean, what do I love to do?' I persisted
and finally she said, 'I love to sail, and I love to travel.' So I
told her about a company in St. Louis, called Intrav, that takes
people around Europe and the Soviet Union on trips. I had
worked with a client in St. Louis who went to work for that
company. She said, 'You mean that's a real job?' I said, 'Yeah!'
So she went off to the library to do some digging—and she
never showed up for her next appointment.

"I finally heard what had happened. After our meeting she
had heard that there was a boat called the *Victory Chimes* that
had been sold and was going to be taken from Duluth back to
the East Coast. She found out who was involved with it and
got herself a job on that boat. She had never thought that it
was possible to connect what she loved with her work."

This kind of creative goal brainstorming is what many of us
do like breathing. But what happens when someone comes in
who's trying to choose a goal in a field you don't understand
at all?

One man came to see me because his high-echelon job was
melting out from under him and he needed to find another
one. The field he was in was one I knew nothing about; he
worked in high finance. His language was full of terminology
about banks and brokerage houses, leveraged buyouts, buying
and selling money to foreign countries. He spoke of small,
prestigious real-estate firms and large supermarket-type investment houses.

So I asked the question I always ask when I'm confronting
the expert:

—"What are the obvious solutions to this problem, and why haven't you tried them?"

He liked that question, and before twenty minutes had passed, he'd given me a very lucid tour of his career path options. I let him teach me. Now we had a place to start from, and we could talk about the issues I do know about: what he liked and didn't like about each of his options, and why; whether he was the kind of man who'd feel more comfortable working for a company, starting his own business, or consulting; and not least of all, how the completely unexpected shock of losing his job at age forty-two might be temporarily clouding his ability to make a choice.

Troubleshooting

Once a client (or friend) has a goal—whether it's one you brainstormed together or one she came in with—she may still have no idea how to begin pursuing it, so to her it's still impossible. Here's the second place where your ingenuity as a brainstorming partner is needed.

The first question is:

—"What's the problem?"

It's important for her to be the one to state the problem, no matter how obvious it may seem to you. For example, one client of mine wanted to paint but said he had too many time commitments. When pressed he finally admitted that he was not being bold enough. By that he meant that he'd been too cautious in his painting and felt he didn't deserve time because he wasn't really serious. The obstacle wasn't as obvious as I thought.

Another question I use in troubleshooting brainstorming is:

—"What would the perfect solution be?"

The answer to this question can reveal your client's frame of reference and save you both a lot of time by defining the issues.

As an alternative, you might want to use LaVaun Maier's problem-identifying exercise. Have the client draw himself in the lower left-hand corner of a sheet of paper, the goal in the upper right-hand corner, and then quickly sketch the obstacles in between. For complete instructions, see p. 18.

Working from the real obstacles, it's much clearer what the possible solutions might be. Then your skills as a problem-solver will easily swing into action, and you can start dreaming up workable solutions to each problem. You might:

—teach the client time-management techniques
—suggest that he interview an admired role model
—help figure out ways to slash costs ("Lyrics a la Carte" did their first nursing-home concert tours in cities where they had friends or relatives, who put them up and lent them a car)
—and in general, have fun shooting obstacles full of holes with the buckshot of good ideas.

Resourcing

Inseparable from troubleshooting is *resourcing*—providing names, organizations, book titles, and other leads. As a professional you've got to become a first-rate resource person.

Being a resource person is partly just a way that some people's minds work. When I meet people I ask them lots of questions, then squirrel away their phone numbers and areas of expertise in my Rolodex, just in case. I also mentally file away odd bits of information I happen to read in magazines, newspapers, and books, and they pop into my head like magic when they're needed. But you can also be quite systematic:

—Clip and file articles with promising information
—Keep a pen handy while you watch TV and note down names, organizations, and book titles
—Collect business cards and phone numbers
—Read want ads

—Go to the library and read the trades—magazines for each profession

—Ask people at social gatherings how they came to do what they're doing

—Read catalogues for local schools

—Read business magazines, artists' magazines, etc., and idea magazines like *Money, Working Woman, New Woman, Entrepreneur, Success, Modern Maturity, Mother Earth News*

—Visit bookstores every chance you get and look at the new titles in Business, Self-Help, and Reference

To organize all the information you're gathering for quick access:

—Open a resource bank—a file organized alphabetically by topic. You can add new topics at any time (if you meet a violin maker, take his card, and start a Musical Instruments category)

That way, if a client says, "I want to know how to get a literary agent," or "I want to find my son a pen pal in China," you can offer leads from your resource bank, or call a contact or a friend for ideas.

Whether you're counseling other people on their careers and personal dreams or simply trying for your own, two heads are better than one. Something powerful happens when you tell someone your dream. And the power increases as you increase the numbers. The more heads and hearts you involve, the more ideas and energy you'll get. When you know how to bring in one friend, you've got the basic building block of support. Now you're ready to start raising that structure.

4 •••

Small Groups and Personal Networks

If telling one person was a significant stride toward your dream, be ready for serious progress when you tell ten or fifteen! Depending on how you prefer to work, you can either contact people one by one, or get them all together in one room. I call the first technique grassroots networking and the second group brainstorming.

The simplest, most informal kind of grassroots networking just adds together the building blocks Help Level 1 began with. When you have a dream or goal, and problems keeping you from getting it, why stop at telling just one person?

GRASSROOTS NETWORKING 1: TELL EVERYONE YOU KNOW.

—Whenever you make a phone call, run into a friend, have coffee with a colleague, tell him about your dream. Ask for ideas.

"Tell everyone you know" may sound obvious, but you'd be surprised how many people are silent about their wishes and works-in-progress, feeling that they have to present their friends with a *fait accompli*. They don't know what they're missing. If you'd like a dazzling demonstration of the power of *Teamworks!* for a minimal investment of time, effort, and organization, start telling people, and watch what happens.

A small example:

The director of publicity for a university press was taking her summer vacation in Yugoslavia. She wanted to take along a Serbo-Croatian phrasebook, so she could say good morning to people in their own language. A search of several bookstores and the local library turned up nothing. As a last resort, she mentioned the problem to her colleagues in the office, doubting that anyone would know where to find such a book. Within a few days, not one but two different Serbo-Croatian phrase-books were on her desk.

You may think you don't know anyone with the special knowledge you need, but you'll be amazed at what the most unlikely people come up with. So:

—Ask everyone. Don't only ask people you think will know. Remember, experts are sometimes experts on what can't be done.

A writer I know needed to find a job for an engineer friend in Eastern Europe, so that she could bring him to America on a work visa. She'd tracked down some Eastern European immigrants in the engineering field, and they'd told her, "It can't be done. You're out of touch with reality." Because the problem was constantly on her mind, she mentioned it at her health club one day. Two dancers (!) became interested. It turned out that one of them was supporting herself by doing word processing at an engineering center. Another's father had imported skilled workers from Eastern Europe for his furniture factory. He knew all about work visas. Through these leads, she got important information that helped her get her friend a job—with her boyfriend's best friend's brother-in-law's brother, thanks to telling everyone she knew.

"One of the biggest things I learned during this project," says Andrea, who created the singing team "Lyrics a la Carte," "was that there's no way we could've done it without net-working. The main thing I found was talking—just talking nonstop about the project, whenever I got a chance—people would overhear me and say, 'Oh yeah! My grandmother's in this home.' So I told all my friends what I was doing, and when I rode the subway I'd purposely have my brochure visible just in case, and I just blathered incessantly to every single person I met, no matter how unlikely it seemed. Sometimes the people you think are going to know everything don't know anything, and the most unexpected people know things.

"I tried to make our first brochure by myself, with our Macintosh computer. I'd taken some graphic design classes. And I just couldn't do it. So this friend suddenly appeared out of the woodwork and helped me with the logo. A directory of nursing homes was suggested by someone where I work. Another woman, in accounting, overheard me talking about it and said, 'Oh! I've been researching nursing homes in Florida for the past month. My mother's going to Florida.' So she gave me a list of homes in Florida. I went to the Foundation Center, where you research grants, and found it really intimidating. I was sitting there with my head in my hands and books piled up around me, and someone came up who I hadn't seen in five years, who's now working as a specialist in getting grants for the arts! *That* kind of weird thing, that's what I mean. She just appeared, sat down with me and said, 'This is the best book to use. Forget about this one.' That just kept happening and happening the whole time. And I found that people really like it when you ask for their advice. Often nobody has asked them before. They're very flattered."

One friend of mine, after searching databases to find information about an obscure illness for another friend of mine, asked me to thank her for letting him be helpful.

A true master of grassroots networking, cellist Ruth S., tells how a very elaborate goal—in this case, a major chamber music festival—can be put together using no other tool than the telephone. Ruth started from scratch six years ago. "I'm a very good cellist, but I had dreams for my career that I thought were only fantasies, that I saw no way of ever doing. All these nice supportive people [experts, no doubt!] were telling me it couldn't be done. Music is such a youth-oriented field. If you're over 25, you have to find a niche, an angle for getting back in again. You can't just do it by winning contests."

Ruth read *Wishcraft*, then brought eight friends to me and said, "Here's a group. Make us a Success Team." We did just that, for eight weeks. When it ended, she took off like a rocket on her own. She had learned two things from the team experience that were enough to excite her. One of them was to try combining more than one of her loves/talents (see What would you be doing in Paradise?, above, p. 36) into a goal. "I'm good at a lot of things," she says. "I organized my team, and I organized a chess club, but I never saw the connection between playing the cello and being an organizer." Ruth came up with the goal of organizing a chamber music series at the private school where her son was a student—and playing in it! "This was everything, all in one."

The second thing Ruth got from the team, and the element that really transformed her life, was telling everybody. She was able to make obstacles shrink dramatically simply by talking to people about what she was doing. "I've been running the chamber music series for about three years now, and very successfully," says Ruth. "But I'd been thinking that I really want to do a festival. There are festivals all over, and I had been hoping against hope that someone would ask me to run one. Finally I realized that instead of waiting, I could do it myself!" Ruth took the first step: she told a friend. "A clarinetist who's the artistic director of a chamber music organization was at my house for dinner one night, and I told him. He said 'It's easy. Find a beautiful place and do it!' And on those words, bells started ringing.

"I wanted a place within one hour's trip of New York City. On May 6 a friend and I started looking, and by June 1 we were ready to go to a contract at a wonderful school. Here, in brief, is how we did it.

"Through my connections at my son's school, I found somebody who'd graduated from a school in Connecticut. Within twenty-four hours I had an appointment with the headmaster of that school. He wasn't interested in having a music festival, but I said, 'What schools do you think *might* be interested?' and he gave me a list. I said, 'Can I say that you suggested I call?' and he said, 'Of course.' So very quickly I got to headmasters, because I was using his name. The school that's going to do the festival was one of the ones he suggested.

"Then I went to my son's headmaster, who is very influential in the private-school world, and I said, 'Will you write a letter of recommendation?' He said, 'Sure.' I said, 'I'll tell you what, I'll write the letter. Will you sign it?' You see, I learned that you have to get the questions, the favor you're asking for, down to the smallest possible detail. And you *also* have to ask a question that can be answered by yes or no. If you go to somebody and say 'I need help,' they'll say, 'Sure, honey, I wish I could,' but if you say, 'I need you to call so-and-so on Tuesday, will you do that?' they either will say yes or they'll say no. If they say no, you thank them and say 'Do you know someone who will?'. If they say yes, you call on Wednesday to see if they did it. You wouldn't believe how good I've gotten at this, and I never knew how to ask anybody for anything before.

"The first annual festival took place at a prestigious West-chester boarding school, and consisted of six Sunday concerts in June. The school has a 450-seat air-conditioned, beautiful auditorium, ninety-four acres, manicured lawns for catered picnics. If I had planned this, if I had designed what I wanted, I couldn't even have come close to what I got."

Six years ago a cellist with an "impossible" dream, today Ruth S. has created an entire music festival. But she's not stopping there. "We travel in France a lot, and I've been wanting to do a festival in a chateau for years," she said. "I told a woman who writes cookbooks that I want to do a festival in a chateau, and I said, 'I'm mentioning it because you lived in France for a while.' She said, 'I know just the person.' Within twenty-four hours, my whole family was invited to a chateau in Burgundy!"

Her friends call Ruth S. "the Queen of the Networkers." Once in motion, she generated her own ideas and energy like a snow-ball rolling downhill. But that's because grassroots networking was the right team technique for her personality.

Not all of us are so courageous and persistent on our own. I'm not. I need to have some humans in the room with me when I'm about to sail off on an odyssey. I like the way energy builds in a room when other people are brainstorming my goal. It means I don't always have to push to keep the ball rolling. Every once in a while I can just sit back and feel taken care of—the ultimate luxury. If you're like me, try this one:

GROUP BRAINSTORMING 1:
THE IDEA/RESOURCE PARTY

An idea/resource party is one of the best parties you'll ever attend or give. It's a small, intimate gathering of friends for the purpose (and the fun) of brainstorming each other's dreams.

—Have your idea/resource party on a weekend evening, or for Sunday brunch. Those seem to be the best times.

—*Do not* invite only people with expertise in the field of your goal/problem. When I threw an idea/resource party for Andrea R., I didn't invite any other singers. There are teams designed for people all in the same field (see Guilds, p. 201, and Mentor/Apprentice Teams, p. 208, but a group brainstorming usually isn't one of them.

—Invite two kinds of friends:

—People who are imaginative and resourceful

—People who have dreams of their own on the back burner

—Invite your friends to bring friends.

—Have no fewer than three people—the minimum team for small-group brainstorming.

—You can have as many as you can comfortably fit in your living room.

—Ask people to bring food.

This last item is important. You can't have a sit-down dinner. It's got to be potluck, buffet style. Everybody has to bring something, and everybody has to help serve. First of all, this establishes informality. When people bring things, they don't mind sitting on the floor. Secondly, it establishes equality and trust. Nobody's a guest in someone else's house, and they're all recipients of each other's gifts. And third, it means everybody's already stuck their neck out in a safe way by presenting something of theirs to the group.

—Give everyone pencils and paper.

—Find out how many people have goals/problems to brainstorm.

Not everyone will have a request. Some people may come just because you throw the best parties. (My friends love these evenings and encourage me to have them more often.) Others will come just to check this idea out, to see if it really works before trying it themselves.

—Divide the available time among goals. Twenty minutes each is about right.

If, during the party, a brainstormer changes his mind and wants to be a brainstormee, but there's not enough time, he gets to throw the next party.

—Follow the basic brainstorming guidelines on p. 33 (include dumb or crazy ideas; write every idea down; find something useful in each idea; improve the useless part).

Note: encourage playfulness. Laughter stimulates brainstorming. Other kinds of socializing (talking about the kids, the movies, the dog) distract from the purpose of this meeting. Despite its festive atmosphere, this is a business meeting, for a business you must take seriously: your own fulfillment. Brainstorming requires undivided attention.

—When brainstorming your goal, let someone else be your writing buddy, and have him write down all the ideas for you. See to it that each brainstormee has a scribe.

It's just part of that atmosphere of being taken care of. A friend is less likely to pre-edit or censor your idea list. You're going to be too busy listening to the ideas—and maybe even putting up an argument—to get them all written down.

Idea/resource (I&R) parties are so helpful, and so much fun, that they may become a regular feature of your social life. And the people who love to come to them can become regulars in your creative network. For example, Donna H., an artist, hosted informal networking gatherings that she called Elegant Evenings for Exceptional Women. Whenever she met another exceptional woman, she'd add her name to the invitation list, and she invited her friends to bring friends. Donna acquired a fascinating assortment of business cards, quite a few new friendships—and a talent pool of people she can call on whenever she or a friend needs information, contacts, or a brainstorming team.

GROUP BRAINSTORMING 2: BUILDING A TALENT POOL

—Start a separate address book of people who come to your idea/resource parties, or who you'd like to invite.
—Beside each one's name, note down what they do and any special skills, experience, or interests.
Examples: Phylliss H., 446-2309. Art director, gourmet cook, newsletter editor, scuba diver.
Sara C., M.D., 260-5673. Sports medicine, history buff. Built own house. Horseback riding.
Richard J., 369-2210. Owns lumberyard, adopted Korean baby, photography, country music.
—Whenever you need an idea squad, or know someone who does, you can assemble one on short notice.

My team doesn't meet regularly anymore. But when I have an idea for a new project, I call a team meeting. Or when I've hit an obstacle, I call a team meeting. And when my courage has flagged and I don't believe the project can work, I call a team meeting.

How can I call a team meeting anytime I want if I don't have a team? I always have a team. It's made up of anybody I can get to come. I call some of the twenty-five people I know who love to brainstorm, and if there's somebody special I want in that team—I know a couple of people who are really great at it—I pick the time to suit them. Remember, a team doesn't have to be more than three people.

* * *

There's a special kind of team meeting I call when I've got to get something done—writing a résumé or stuffing envelopes for a newsletter. This kind of team meeting—in which five or ten people pitch in to get an actual task done for one person —is none other than an old-fashioned barn-raising.

AN OLD-FASHIONED BARN-RAISING

This differs from a brainstorming in that:

- —The objective of the party is to get an actual task completed by its end.
- —The best time is often an afternoon.
- —This time, you provide the food and drink in exchange for help and company.
- —This is not an idea party, but an action party (though ideas may be part of the action if, for instance, the purpose is to get a first-rate résumé or inquiry letter written and typed).
- —For physical tasks, concentration is less sacrosanct—you can put on a movie or music.

The kinds of tasks that can be tackled and vanquished by a barn-raising know no bounds. I knew one woman whose goal was to feel beautiful: she had four friends take her shopping and teach her to put on makeup. Almost anything you've been putting off because it's intimidating or just plain boring is a likely candidate for a barn-raising. If you know a friend or family member who's been complaining about some task undone, you can produce a barn-raising for him. It makes a great surprise or birthday party.

Got a stubborn or interesting problem? Want to draw on an even wider pool of ideas and resources? Love getting mail?

Here's a simple way to expand a local talent pool into a nationwide mail network, for a start-up cost of under $15 in postage:

GRASSROOTS NETWORKING 2: POSTCARD PROBLEMSHOOTERS

—At the end of an idea/resource party, ask each participant to think of the five or six people they know all over the country who might love brainstorming.

—Put together a list of twenty-five to thirty names and addresses.

Don't just write and ask if each person want to be part of a brainstorming network. They won't know what they're saying yes or no to. Send a problem the very first time, to turn them on.

—Write (and photocopy) a short letter about the goal and problem in question. (Add a handwritten note letting each recipient know how you got his/her name.)

Be as specific as you can about what you need ("I'm looking for a blue pickup truck with no wheels for under $200"), but also tell why you need it ("I'm putting on a Sam Shepard play and need it for the stage set").

—Tell your story—what you want to accomplish, what you've already done, and what you haven't been able to do.

—Ask for ideas.

—Include the target date for the answer.

—Enclose a self-addressed, stamped postcard or envelope.

—On the back of your letter or the blank side of the postcard, at the bottom, write: "I would enjoy being part of the problem-solving network again," with two boxes, marked Yes and No. And: "I would like to put a problem of my own into the network," with a space to describe the problem.

—Ask for additional names to add to the list.

This technique can also be used locally, for an intensive search of any kind—if you're looking for a job, skill, resource, professional service, house, apartment, kitten, etc. Send postcards to everyone you can think of, telling them what you need and when you need it. (Postcards can be done on a copy machine.) "I wanted to move out of my apartment," says Andrea R. of "Lyrics a la Carte" fame. "My budget was incredibly low, and I couldn't find anything. So I wrote a form letter, made fifty copies, and sent it to everybody I know in New York. It was like a bulk mailing—a friendly letter with little pictures. 'I really want to move. If you know of anything, please tell me.' Lots of people called and gave me leads, and I found a place. It was really effective."

If you find brainstorming-by-mail fun and productive, and you've got even four or five correspondents who like it as much as you do, your postcard problemshooters network is already evolving into . . . a newsletter.

YOUR OWN NETWORK NEWLETTER

A personal newsletter doesn't have to be professionally typeset, or appear like clockwork once a month. It can be typed, copied, and sent out whenever you feel like it. It enables the members of the problemshooters network to talk to each other, as well as to you. The payoff is a sense of community-by-mail and periodic mental workouts for people who enjoy the game of problem-solving.
There are three things you can put in your newsletter:

Success Stories from previous networkings.
—"I asked you all for a blue pickup truck with no wheels. Sara J. from N.J. got one from her son's friend who collects junked cars. Mary W. from N.H. has a trucker cousin who brought it here for me. The play goes on at Central High School September 30, and the set is fabulous. Thanks!"

Brain Busters, which are either requests for leads or solutions to the previous requests.

Q: "J.S. of Fort Myers Beach, Florida, wants to start a beauty contest for women over 40. Wants to know: has there ever been such a contest? When? Where? Who to contact/where to read about it? Needs info about organizing beauty pageants in general; where to advertise for contestants, get publicity."

A: "A.G. of New York heard about a beauty contest for women over 30. A January issue of L.A. *Times* Sunday Magazine had a cover story on 'The Obsession: the L.A. Body' that mentioned the contest. Also: for publicity, try *Vogue* and the new *Lear's* magazine 'for the woman who wasn't born yesterday' (i.e., over 40). *Lear's* might want to cover or even sponsor your contest, especially if the 'beauty' was more than skin deep."

Skills and needs exchange. This is a swap system.

—"Maria K. of Dubuque, Iowa, will do support backup for most computers for anyone in the network for $15 an hour—a great value. Needs brochure and business card design—buy or barter."

—"Ralph M. of Portland seeks radical concepts for graphics book. Will offer photo services."

There are many variations on this system. For example, in her eight-page newsletter, *Resource Sharing,* Meta H. of Eugene, Oregon, combined the brain busters and skills and needs features into a simple page divided into two columns: "Resource Sharing: Offerings" and "Resource Sharing: Requests."

Newsletter participants need a simple system for contacting each other. *You* need a way to cover copying and mailing costs.

—Since this is a private network, people may be willing to put in their names and addresses or phone numbers; *or:*

—Some may prefer to sign "M.K., Dubuque, Iowa." Responses then are sent to you as "editor/publisher" and can be printed in the next newsletter; *or:* charge a dollar for each request, and forward the answers.

—The first newsletter can be sent to new participants free. (Ask network members to send you addresses of interested friends.)

—Place this announcement at the end: "If you'd like to keep getting this newsletter, please send $2 for the next four issues, to cover postage and copying costs." (Average cost of a one- or two-page newsletter, per recipient: copying, 15–30 cents; postage, 25 cents.)

As an alternative, you might want to publish your costs and invite donations, as Meta H. did. Her "Resource Sharing" newsletter was typed, beautifully laid out with illustrations, and photocopied. On page 7, under "Open books," she printed the costs of her newsletter, which totaled $110 for 200 copies. And under "Do you want to see more newsletters?" there were eight suggestions for reader participation, one of which is, "Send money. This is a very concrete method of encouragement."

Production methods and design of personal newsletters vary widely. Though mine really was in the professional newsletters category (see below), I just typed it, pasted on the *Wishcraft* or *Teamworks!* logo, and copied it on both sides of the page— reducing it so I could use more material. But I've seen some that are handsome examples of desktop publishing.

Note: As with other team techniques in this book, your newsletter may grow and establish itself, or it may peter out after three issues. A lot depends on you: how much you're getting out of it, how much time and energy you want to put into it. Don't feel like a failure if your newsletter (or team, or I&R party circuit) doesn't go on forever. Simply having used any of the *Teamworks!* systems once will revolutionize your way of doing things. And you can start them up again anytime you need them.

The network newsletter is one in the package of services you can offer if you want to have your own business as a career developer or *Wishcraft/Teamworks!* counselor (see p. 162).

A professional's network newsletter is like the personal newsletter described above in that it can feature success stories, brain busters, and a skills and needs exchange. But it's different in some key respects. For one thing, you'll probably want to produce a newsletter at regular intervals, and you may want to take more care than I did with layout and design. Since the newsletter is advertising for you and your brainstorming skills, you may want to feature a brainstorming column in which *you* offer solutions to problems sent in by one or more network members, to show your abilities as an idea person.

You'll also solicit newsletter contributors in a more deliberate and systematic way than the informal editor-publishers of personal newsletters. At the end of every *Teamworks!* seminar you give (they'll be explained in chapter 8), invite participants to join your network by filling out 3 × 5 cards. On their cards they will write:

—Name, address, and phone number
—Skills
—Needs

Besides getting the addresses of potential subscribers, you now have material for a skills and needs exchange that can become a valuable part of your resource bank (p. 42), as well as a column in the newsletter. If you're a real bear for organization, you can file names alphabetically or by seminar. (For quick access, I give each person a number, beginning with a code for the date and place of their seminar. For example: "4/12/9 HI 14" is the fourteenth name on the list of participants from the April 12, 1989, seminar at the Holiday Inn.) And cross-index them to an alphabetical list of skills (Carpentry, Catering, Circus, Diet, Dogs, etc.). This is easier if you have a personal computer, though there's much to be said for the old-fashioned card file.

Send each seminar participant a first, *free* issue of your newsletter, and give each of your individual clients a free copy. Include a subscription coupon: "Would you like to keep receiving this newletter?" Instead of just a subscription, you can offer network membership, with other benefits included in the price, such as a discount on one individual counseling session and personal access to the skills and needs exchange, that is, being put directly in touch with other network members who can serve their needs or need their services. Include a coupon in the newsletter for the name and address of a friend who might enjoy this newsletter. Send the friend a free copy.

Besides being extraordinarily helpful to readers, this newsletter is a tool that can help you build your clientele.

Earlier, I talked about the energy that multiplies as more and
more people join in a group brainstorming/barn-raising. By just
calling a friend on the phone, you've broken the spell of isolation. It's even better when you've got four friends over, helping you write your résumé or coming up with suggestions for
your first job interview. But you haven't seen anything until
you've brainstormed with a roomful of people in an auditorium,
gym, or community hall.

5...

Large-Group Brainstorming

When you put 40 or 80 or 120 heads together, it seems there is no problem that you cannot solve, given time and some simple techniques for tapping into hidden resources. Consider the Small World Experiment, conducted by psychologist Stanley Milgram.

Milgram got just twenty strangers into a room with a wallful of telephone books. He said he could get a note hand-delivered anywhere in the United States within three days, just using the resources he had in that room. Somebody with a blindfold picked a telephone book, opened it at random, and put his finger on the name and address of a woman in North Dakota. They started brainstorming how they could get a note to her. It turned out that somebody in the room had a friend whose cousin was a trucker who could get there the next day. That wasn't all. They found eleven other ways in that room of getting the note hand-carried to the woman within three days. That experiment was the origin of the saying, "You're five handshakes away from anyone in the United States." That was done with twenty people. Imagine what fifty or a hundred could do.

Don't pass up an opportunity to brainstorm in a large group. If there's someone in the room who wants to get a short story published, there's a writer in the room who's done it and knows how. If someone stands up and says, "I'd like to produce comic books to sell in China," someone else waves her hand and says, "My brother travels to China on business and is fluent in Chinese." Miracles happen. You wouldn't believe the creative ideas and contacts that any large gathering of people commands, or the energy and excitement created when they realize it. Here's how to make it happen:

LARGE-GROUP BRAINSTORMING 1— ONE PERSON AT A TIME

Ways to get a large group together:

—Offer this event to any regular meeting of any organization you belong to or can get to:
   —church or temple group
   —Junior League
   —alumni(ae) association
   —PTA
   —professional association (invite spouses too)
   —union local
   —singles club
   (The advantage of this method is that you have a guaranteed pool of people to draw on, so you have a good chance of getting a large enough group.)
—Advertise through your local Y or adult-education organization, on posters in neighborhood gathering places, on bulletin boards in your company or school, in learning exchange catalogues, or in your local newspaper, *or*:
—Have everyone in your talent pool or personal network invite five people.

If you are a counseling professional, you have a ready-made pool of people to draw on:
—your clients, if you are an independent career developer (see p. 162)
—company employees, if you are in Human Resource Development (see p. 158)

—students and alumni(ae), if you are high school or college affiliated (see p. 163)

—graduates of your *Wishcraft/Teamworks!* seminars (see Chapter 8)

—members of Success Teams or company dream teams (we'll tell you on p. 158 why we have a separate name for corporate teams)

Here's how I run a large-group brainstorming.

Acting as master of ceremonies, I welcome everyone and explain what's going to happen. Often I'll tell a story about something exciting that happened at the last brainstorming. Then I instruct everyone in the room to think of something she or he really wants—something that isn't easy to get. "Don't go for something lukewarm, something you can take or leave. Miracles are going to happen in this room," I tell them. "Why waste a miracle on something you don't really care about?" Then I discuss the "What do you want/What's the problem" format, and I talk about some of the most common obstacles (you can refer to the list of obstacles on p. 19 if it helps). I explain that they are to take each problem presented to them as a challenge. Turn on the brainpower, and shrink that obstacle, until the person in front of the room can see an open path to her goal.

Now I ask for a volunteer to stand and tell the whole room his wish. (I also pick a scribe and seat him or her beside the volunteer with a pencil and pad of paper.) After he has told his wish, I ask him what the problem is. Then I call for hands from anyone in the room who has a suggestion. I don't want the audience to restrict their ideas to the sensible, workable, or practical, but to use innovative thinking, too, even if it seems farfetched. I tell the scribe to write everything down, without censoring. Pretty soon hands are shooting up, and ideas are starting to come.

When the scribe has written down six to ten ideas, I have the volunteer go through the list and pick out the ideas he or she thinks won't work. This is brainstorming practice. I have him or her find the usable kernel in each of those seemingly useless ideas—and invite the group to help turn that kernel into a new, workable idea. "Never throw away an idea because it seems unworkable," I tell them. "That just means you haven't gotten past the surface, down to where the interesting stuff is. Human beings are genetically incapable of coming up with an idea that has absolutely no merit. You don't throw out the baby, you change the bathwater." This technique is the essential brainstorming follow-up. The ideas come more slowly, but they get better and better. An example will make it clearer how this works.

A woman in one of my seminars was a certified scuba diving instructor who wanted to teach in the Caribbean. Her problem: her boyfriend was a real estate broker in New England, and they didn't want to be apart. That's a typical problem for a two-career couple; when the partners' job opportunities are in different locations, they feel forced to choose between the relationship and the career.

There were over a hundred people in that room, and the group brainstormed for the scuba diver. Among the ideas we came up with were:

1. Get your partner involved in your business—find a way to combine your interests. Resort real estate?
2. Teach in the Caribbean for just two months a year.
3. Teach scuba diving in New England.

Idea 1 seemed promising, but long-range. The woman said she would discuss it with her partner. The problem with idea 2 was that the separation was still too long and the pay would be too low. The good thing about idea 3 was that she could do her work and live with her partner; the problem was, "I don't want to teach scuba diving in New England! There aren't any coral reefs—just cold-water dives to old wrecks." I asked the group, "How do we fix *that* problem?" Solutions started coming up:

—Train scuba divers in New England swimming pools or quarries, then take them on one-week tours to the Caribbean.
—Find someone who owns resorts in the Caribbean and would want to work with you building up diving tours to his resorts.

These were the best ideas yet, but no one had come up with them on the first round of brainstorming. They arose from tryng to fix first-round ideas instead of dismissing them.

After ten minutes of brainstorming for my first volunteer, I call up another person (and pick another scribe to take notes). By this time people are getting energized, and more hands go up when I ask for ideas. I spend a maximum of ten minutes on each person. We can usually brainstorm for five or ten people before the energy in the room starts flagging. I call an intermission, and then we start up for another hour.

This kind of large-group brainstorming is effective because everyone in the room can watch the drama of each problem getting solved. It does wonders for the sense of possibility. As the meeting goes on, more and more people will feel hopeful and want to get up in front of that room with a long-neglected dream.

And that, of course, is a problem: you can't do an individual brainstorming for each of one hundred people. Many people love to come anyway and resolve to be the first to speak next time.

If you had the time, there's no way you wouldn't come up with half a dozen truly workable ideas for every person in the room. But even fifteen people can take over two hours. The result can be a roomful of inspired but frustrated people who didn't get their chance in the sun. That's why I like to combine this kind of group brainstorming with another kind that gives everyone a chance.

LARGE-GROUP BRAINSTORMING 2: THE NETWORKING GAME— EVERYBODY ALL AT ONCE

I also call this the idea bath, and you'll see why. It's a wonderful exercise in creative hysteria that breaks down any lingering inhibitions about asking for help with our goals.

Before I describe the networking game, though, I'd like to say a word or two about networking.

In its best, oldest form, networking is a natural human activity that has gone on forever and always will, because it's both affectionate and efficient. If you help your friend's son get an interview with your wife who's an executive in a bank, everyone concerned feels good about it.

In its eighties form, however, networking has come to have an exploitive tinge, and some of us have gotten wary of it. Some networking gatherings are cocktail parties where you walk around with a glass in one hand and a business card in the other, feeling like you're trying to use people. For real or imagined reasons, it seems like opportunism thinly cloaked with sociability. And because you have to maintain the fiction of sociability by chatting politely before you get to the point, you never meet enough people. Too often these gatherings are neither genuinely sociable nor genuinely useful.

I designed the networking game to bypass that problem. The game is structured so that you will talk to many people—even if you're a born wallflower—and you're not only allowed, but expected, to get to the point at once. Also, you get to help just as many people as help you, so you don't have that secret feeling of being a user. In the game there's no cloaked opportunism—just an honest request for help. But since it's kept to ridiculous time limits, like a hurried scavenger hunt, everyone is breathless and laughing, and the event ends up being as genuinely friendly and festive as it is useful.

The networking game requires some simple materials. I always bring along 3 × 5 cards for everyone in the room, and a box of straight pins for pinning the cards on our shirt fronts. I tell everyone to take out paper and pencil.

Before I start the networking game, I ask at least two or three people to stand up, state a wish and problem, and ask the audience for ideas—a short demonstration of large-group brainstorming one at a time. This makes the room aware of its own resources—and makes everyone eager to get at them! After the demonstration, I pass out the 3 × 5 cards and pins. Everyone is to write on their wish card:

—Name
—Goal ("What do you want?")
—Main obstacle ("What's the problem?")

I ask them to define both goal and obstacle as precisely as possible. If your goal is "to change careers from computers to psychotherapy," and the problem is "I have no training," the other person has a handle to grab.

I tell them to pin their cards to their shirts and have paper and pencil ready. "Now stand up, and pair off with somebody you don't know. When I say 'Go!' you have one minute. Point to your card and say to your partner, 'I want x and the problem is y!' Write down every idea the other person comes up with. Keep that pencil moving! If the person has more information to offer than you can squeeze into one minute, get his or her phone number! . . . Go!"

The room goes wild. You haven't heard noise till you've heard fifty or more people all talking at top speed and top volume (there's no way you can whisper fast). Cocktail parties hardly simmer. This room boils with energy and ideas.

After one minute, I yell, "Switch roles!" and the partner who's been giving ideas asks for them. In reality I've usually lied a little bit about the time limit. I keep my eye on the crowd, and if everyone's talking and scribbling eagerly, I let them continue for as long as two minutes. I want to give them time to come up with some good ideas, but I also want them to believe they haven't got time. Why? Because it's the time pressure that lowers inhibitions and releases energy! When you know the clock is ticking, there's no time to say it nicely, the way you were raised to do. You can't say, "How do you do? How have you been?" You must say, "I want a Porsche. Got any ideas?" It's very funny to be so direct and outspoken, and it's permitted to break social rules in this game—because you've been told to do so.

You also have to get very assertive about finding your next partner. No one is going to set up this date for you. You have to run right up and ask for it, or you're going to waste your next minute wandering around looking for somebody.

When the second minute is up, and the first two partners

have had a complete exchange, I yell, "Change partners!" (By now I'm having major trouble getting people's attention. That's a very good sign.) They have about three seconds to find somebody. I call out, "If you can't find a partner, raise your hand high so someone can find you!" I give the new partners one generous minute each, and then yell "Switch!" again. And so on.

No one gets to talk to everyone in the room, but after ten or fifteen rounds of this madness, everyone's pad of paper is overflowing with ideas and phone numbers. At the end of the game I schedule some free time, so that if someone had more ideas for you than there was time for, or if you suddenly thought of an idea for your first partner when you were talking to your fourth, you can seek each other out and pick up where you left off.

There's a lot more going on in the networking game than just getting information. It breaks down the barriers between strangers, and that makes it a great way to meet people. It also teaches us how to ask. That experience will come in handy every time a step toward your goal involves calling a stranger on the phone. The game also teaches focus and precision of language. It's a crash course in effective communication. By the time you get to the third person, you have a much sharper sense of how to ask for what you want. Even if you came out of the networking game without a single good idea (and I've never seen that happen), you'd still have acquired these valuable skills. Most people come out of the game simply amazed at how energized they feel brainstorming with a roomful of seemingly ordinary people.

Career counseling professionals: Periodic networking meetings are another valuable service that you can offer your clientele—as well as another tool for expanding that clientele, since regulars will bring newcomers. As a format for monthly networking meetings, you can combine both kinds of large-group brainstorming: a demonstration of one-at-a-time brainstorming followed by a networking game.

6...

The Perilous Brink
of Action

Whether you've done your brainstorming with one friend on the phone, or seven at a dinner party, or with 175 people in a big room at the Y, you end up with the same thing: a list of ideas. This is where Help Level 1 of *Teamworks!*—informal support systems—ends and Help Level 2, with its structured support systems, begins.

If ideas are all you need, this is the point at which you put this book down and go out on your own. You'll never be as alone as you were before, because now you know how to call a team—large or small—whenever you run into a snag, need suggestions, or just feel like having some company. But in Help Level 1—with the exception of an occasional barn-raising—the main purpose of your teams has been to give you ideas and leads. Now it's necessary to turn those ideas and leads into actions. And this is the point at which most of us really start needing support.

I'll show you why.

PLANNING TO FIRST STEPS:
THE BRINK OF ACTION

The only way to turn ideas into actions is to work them down to little steps that you can do right away—tomorrow, the next day, the coming week. When it comes to getting dreams on track, next month might as well be never. So what you've got to do now is take your list of ideas, sit down with a piece of paper and a pencil, and choose one you like.

At this point you need to do some backward planning, building a bridge of steps from the goal on your horizon right back to your doorstep. "What do I have to do before I can rent a house by the sea? Obviously, find one for rent that I can afford. What do I have to do before I can do that? Get some newspapers with classified ads for rentals in the right areas. What do I have to do before that? Decide what seacoasts I'm interested in, and find out what the local papers are. How will I find that out? Go to the library and look in a national directory of newspapers. Can I do that this week? Yes." You have to make sure these steps are real and specific—things you can do right away. Write them all down.

Now you've got to get out your pocket calendar and start scheduling those steps. Write them in just like you would dentist appointments, business meetings, and important birthdays. When are you going to make that call? What day do you have time to go to the library? By what date will you have all your inquiry letters written? (Ordinarily, you won't plan any further than two weeks ahead. By the end of that time, you'll have so much new information that you'll need another planning session.) Write as many steps into the week as you think you can really handle—and then add one or two more. You want to be realistic, but just a little rushed. If you expect the impossible of yourself, you're setting yourself up for failure. But if you give yourself too much time, you'll lose the sense of urgency and excitement that you owe to yourself and your cherished goal.

I'll give you two examples. A woman in one of my seminars had as her goal, "To get in shape and become more athletic."

Her problem was finding the time to do it. The steps and schedule she wrote down in the planning stage were:

—go to the health club every day this week
—get a nutritional analysis done
—by Friday: make a list of other gyms to investigate
—next week: call other gyms for info
—choose a new gym

She made it her target, or short-term goal, to walk in the door
of a new gym in a week and a half.

Another woman's goal was to advance in her company. For
the next ten days, she committed herself to researching aspects
of the firm. She knew she'd have to go to the library. That was
easy. But she also made a list of people she should interview,
and in her calendar she wrote down a specific day to approach
each one and make an appointment to sit down and ask questions.

And then she discovered that planning had brought her to
the point where she needed to call in support.

"When I looked at that list, my heart sank," she told me.
"Library research is safe and cozy, but calling George S. the
day after tomorrow at ten, and saying, 'Do you have any time
to see me this week, George?' and having George say yes, is
awfully real."

There are no two things in this world as unrelated to each
other as talking about something and doing it. Talking about
swimming feels nothing at all like swimming. You don't even
get wet. Planning is easy. Research is fun. But now you are getting into the *doing* phase. There are probably a couple of no-risk
things on your planning sheet, such as going to the library and
calling your brother. But there will also be some things on that
sheet that are riskier; things that make your heart beat faster,
and you're not sure whether it's with anticipation or fear.

Habitual actions are calming, reassuring. But whenever you
create, learn, or do something you've never done before, you're
in a high-risk enterprise. These new things can make you catch
your breath. Imagine walking up to a famous person you've
wanted to meet all your life and saying hello. I call them firing-

squad moments. It doesn't matter how small or insignificant they may seem to someone else—for you, they are powerfully important.

Some people thrive on those moments. They are the ones for whom Help Level 1 may be enough. Maybe they're the Evel Knievels among us—people who feel most alive when there's an element of danger. If you are one of those people, you're very lucky. Perhaps you've already had the experience of successfully taking risks: you've won some, lost some, and learned in your bones that it's worth it.

On the other hand, maybe you're like me. I hate danger. Everything in me has been designed for survival. And so when I come to one of those "This is it" moments, I'm likely to say, "I think I'm going home." If you're like me, you'll come up with a great excuse: "I'm not sure it's such a good idea after all. I changed my mind. I'd rather go fishing." Or, you'll make a weak start, look in a couple of newspapers, write one or two letters, even make a phone call—and then the dog will need to go to the vet, your boss will want you to work late, the taxes will be due, and you'll just get very tired. Then you'll wonder why you woke up those wishes again when you can't have them anyway, because they're too hard to get.

You're right. They *are* too hard to get—alone. Ideas and resources are not enough. We also need ongoing support. (If you think you know someone who doesn't need it, look again. I'll bet you she or he already has it.) When you use the full-fledged *Teamworks!* system, getting ideas and leads is only the beginning. The important thing you do is get people to meet with you every week to support you in what you want to do.

That is a Success Team.

PART II
HELP LEVEL 2: BUILDING STRUCTURED SUPPORT SYSTEMS (SUCCESS TEAMS)

7 •••

What Is a Success Team?
And Why Do You Need One?

A Success Team is completely different from any other kind of team you've ever been on before. A computer programmer I know calls it a "paradigm shift" in the concept of teams. What he means is this: ordinary teams submerge individuality for the sake of a common goal. They're designed so people can pull together to reach a target outside the team, a project or a touchdown. A Success Team's goal is to have everyone pull together to reach a target *inside* the team: to make sure that each member gets his or her personal goal.

Once you've revealed your dream, your team will not let you forget it. As my own first team told me, "Sher, this time you're going to get what you want whether you want it or not!" A Success Team has been called "an affectionate bunch of asskickers." They'll let you go at your own pace, but they will not let you chicken out. And they won't let all the things that have stopped you in the past—setbacks, low moods, daily demands, and interruptions—stop you again.

A brainstorming of the kind described in the last section can get you all fired up and ready to go. A Success Team will *keep* you going, steadily, step by step, week after week, through all the gritty little details and snags, the heart-stoppers, the slow spots—until one day, with or without a "positive attitude," whether or not you have "self-discipline," or "believe in yourself," you arrive right in the middle of your goal. You own your house, you're riding your horse, you're opening your own shop, working with wildlife, showing up for your exciting new job, or you've gotten your acceptance letter to a great college.

All it really ever takes to reach your goal is perseverance—that's true. But we think of perseverance as an individual character trait, a virtue. It isn't. All the word means is "keeping going," the way you show up for work or school, or babies, or just for dinner—because you have to—because someone is expecting you, or depending on you. That homely, overlooked little fact is the secret of success. A Success Team puts it to work for your personal dreams.

Maybe you've let fear (or its favorite disguise, fatigue) stop you in the past. There are two perfectly good reasons to feel fear when you're going for what you love. One is that you've run into something that you don't know how to do. The other is that you're having stage fright.

Your Success Team will take the first kind of fear very seriously. It will help you to inform yourself, rehearse, and prepare. But the second kind of fear, stage fright, is healthy and normal. If you're not afraid of some of the steps you're taking, you're not taking big enough steps. You're supposed to be anxious when you're doing something important. But you are not supposed to quit. So your Success Team will not take your stage fright seriously. They will cheer you on and encourage you to throw a first-class negativity tantrum, and then they'll say, "That was good! Now, do it!" If necessary, they'll hold your hand all the way to the job interview or audition. And they'll wait to hear how it went.

But what about setbacks? From a minor dead end ("No one will talk to me at that agent's office") to a major disaster ("My project was totally rejected, and the client doesn't even like me anymore!"), setbacks are as inevitable as taxes. The crucial difference between being a winner and a loser is how you respond to them. As we all know, if you keep getting up from the canvas no matter how many times you're knocked down, you're bound to win. You don't need to be told that. But how do you find the hope, heart, and energy to keep getting back up? Talk is cheap. "Get up," like "Cheer up," is just a pair of words. The feeling inside when you've been knocked on the canvas once too often is much bigger than a slogan. When you've had a setback, what can a Success Team offer you besides words?

Something mysteriously important: continuity. Simple ongoingness. Just promise yourself you'll show up at your team meeting every week. That's all. Help your teammates, and rest awhile. After a few sessions you'll feel ready to start moving again. And then you'll find that your team has held your goal in trust for you. When you hit a snag working alone, the impetus tends to get buried and forgotten. By the time your energy and optimism come back, you might be doing something else.

Your Success Team will be waiting for you every week, the way your job waits for you to come in in the morning and your kids wait for you to make dinner at night. That's the normal machinery of life. It keeps you going no matter how you feel. Except that the machinery called Success Teams is for you.

So to fulfill your dream, you don't have to become one of those rare people (so rare I've never met one) who never feel defeated. You can go toward your beloved goal the same way you go on living day to day—good and bad, slow and fast, terrific and lousy, cheerful and peppy, sloppy and sleepy. Continuity of structure, continuity of support—not attitude or character—is the key to keeping going, and keeping going is the *major* secret of getting there.

Where do you think you'd be if you'd had that kind of support all your life? In a very different place than you are now?

What if, at the end of a week of action, you were going to meet with four people who were eagerly waiting to hear the results? Would it make a difference?

If you've ever had trouble sticking to a course of action that was just for you, or if the thing you'd really love to do seems just too hard to get, create a Success Team.

Here's how:

—First, you'll need to find people who are also interested in having a Success Team behind them, and who would make enthusiastic, committed teammates (Chapter 8: Finding Your Team, Part 1: The *Wishcraft/Teamworks!* Seminars and Chapter 9: Finding Your Team, Part 2: On Your Own).

—Once you find them, you need to know how to weld
that group of friends—or strangers—into a working team
(Chapter 10: How to Run a Success Team, the First Meeting: Team-Building).
—And finally, you need instructions for keeping your team
running smoothly, so that each of you gets first-rate help
and support (Chapter 11: The Second Meeting: Goal-
Setting, Chapter 12: The Third—and All Subsequent
Meetings, and Chapter 13: Team Troubleshooting).

Once you're familiar with the basic Success Team design, I'll
tell you some Success Stories (Chapter 14) of dreams people
have achieved with the support of their teams. And then, in
the final section of the book, we'll go on to explore some of the
most successful Variations on a Team, from corporate Dream
Teams to family Home Teams to Senior Success Teams—and
more.

A PRELIMINARY NOTE
ON FINDING YOUR TEAM

When you hear people talk about their Success Team
teammates—people they've known for maybe six months or a
year—you'd think they were talking about lifelong friends. "The
four of us just went out to celebrate a year together," Jim S.,
a Boston software salesman, told me. "I can't imagine the team
with even one of us missing. Each person is so vital to our
particular chemistry." "We've become fast friends, and gotten
to know and trust each other in very intimate and direct ways,"
actor/director Derek C. said when his team had been meeting
for eighteen months. A good Success Team experience is so
nourishing to each individual, and so bonding for the group,
that teammates can quickly become some of the most important
people in your life. So you probably have to exercise enormous
care in choosing your teammates in the first place. Right?
    Guess again.
Some of the most successful and long-lasting teams have

started out as four strangers who just happened to be sitting near each other at one of my *Wishcraft/Teamworks!* seminars. Other great teams have started by putting a "Success Team forming" notice on a bulletin board, or in a bookstore window, and informally interviewing whoever calls. Of course, some teams are made up of co-workers or friends. But the point is that you don't have to undertake an arduous talent search for the perfect teammates. Almost any four or five interested people can become a team—and once you are a working team, you'll probably be convinced that by some act of Providence, you've found the perfect teammates!

This happens because Success Teams tap into the part of people that's both most universal and most individual—the part that hopes and dreams, imagines and creates. When you meet that part of someone—and the team-building exercises coming up in Chapter 10 are especially designed to make the introduction—you usually can't help being fascinated and moved. No matter who the person is, you can sympathize with his or her dreams—because you have dreams of your own— yet each person turns out to be so different, so unique! Many people have told me that they sat down at a *Teamworks!* seminar thinking the people around them were boring, or not their type, and that an hour later, those same people had opened up and turned into some of the most amazing people they've ever met in their life. Under the right circumstances, you can make that kind of discovery about almost anyone. A Success Team will create the circumstances. You just have to find the people. The next two chapters will show you how to do just that.

8...

Finding Your Team, Part 1: The *Wishcraft/Teamworks!* Seminars

The easiest way to find a team for yourself is to sign up for a *Wishcraft/Teamworks!* seminar, if they are available in your area.

A seminar gives you a taste of how powerful it is to work on a dream with a buddy, with a seminar Success Team, and with an ongoing Success Team. The advantage of a seminar is that it puts you right in the middle of a large group of people who are actively seeking teammates, and with a seminar leader who will guide you through the team-building process. If she is following my plan for a package of career-counseling services (p. 162), she may also coach new teams after the seminar, for their first several meetings.

Since one of my goals and a purpose of this book is to teach the designs for the *Teamworks!* seminars, to encourage career counselors and human-resources trainers to run them, the likelihood that you can find the seminars in your area is good. If you can't find someone who's giving them, show this book to a career counselor, teacher, psychologist, or just plain talented event-organizer, and persuade him to run one. Or maybe you are a talented event-organizer who enjoys working with people. Those are the only requirements for running a *Wishcraft/Teamworks!* seminar. Go to your local Y, church, or social-service or professional organization, and propose that they let you run one. Just for inspiration, here's a partial list of organizations I've run seminars for:

—Associations of Women Business Owners in a number of states (call the National Association in Washington, DC)

—American Institute of Musical Studies (in Austria!)

—Philadelphia Women in Communications

—National Network of Graduate Business School Women

—YWCA of Chicago, Minneapolis, Rochester, New York, Champaign-Urbana, and many others

—University women's organizations

—Interface Educational Center, Watertown, Massachusetts

—The Learning Exchange, New York City

—Babson College Alumni Association

—Executive Woman

—National Secretaries Association International

—Women in Publishing

—The American Booksellers' Association

—For the Sports Minded (a singles' organization)

—JFK University Summer Institute for Career Developers, Orinda, California

—Sales and Marketing Executives International

—Fayetteville, North Carolina, Junior League

—an electronics firm

—the City of New York

—Bronx Women's NOW

—Flight Attendants' Union, San Francisco

—The Unitarian Church

—The Army Corps of Engineers

—Sarah Lawrence College

as well as Fortune 500 companies.

There have been many others, but I want you to notice the variety, the unexpected on my list, and see if it tickles your imagination. Other ideas: the PTA, any retirees' organization or senior center, Parents Without Partners, Weight Watchers, AA or Al-Anon, the Chamber of Commerce . . . the garden club!

You may have noticed the predominance of the word "women" in my list of organizations. Women were the original market for Success Team seminars. They were more willing than men to admit that they needed support. Also, they'd been giving support to men and children for years—and they jumped at the chance to get some for themselves. This is changing. Men find that they love the seminars and Success Teams once they get in them, but they're a little more resistant to signing up. Women's groups are still one of the most responsive markets for this seminar. Some other groups that are receptive:

— *Singles, divorcees, the widowed, and the recently relocated*— because they're looking for productive and interesting ways to meet quality people. (I like to hear that people use my seminars to make friends or become part of a new community. It's so much more humane and ac- curate to assess people on the basis of what's inside them—their dreams, their personal style—rather than on how they look or how clever they are at first en- counters.)

— *Career changers*—both those in mid-career and reentry women. They're taking a big risk and need extra sup- port.

— *Freelancers and fledgling entrepreneurs*—people who work alone and don't have the structure of an office and a boss to support and motivate them.

— *Gifted underachievers*—that probably includes most of you. It means anyone who has more talent inside him than he's using.

— *Recent college graduates*—first-time entry into the world of work can be extraordinarily stressful and lonely. A certain amount of rejection is almost inevitable, and very hard to take alone. For young people in this situation, Success Teams are lifesavers.

Organizing and promoting a seminar is a big job—especially the first time. If it's too daunting a task to take on alone, don't let that stop you. Put together a Create-an-Event Team (p. 194) to help you do it. It's worth the effort. A *Wishcraft/Teamworks!* seminar is an exciting event—one that often increases mem- bership and attendance for organizations that sponsor it, and gives independent career counselors the high profile they need to attract a clientele. Local newspapers, TV, and radio are often interested in covering the seminar—and the person who gives it—if informed in advance by telephone or press release. Be my guest and call it a *Wishcraft*/*Teamworks!* seminar if you like, to capitalize on name recognition. (If you want to do something in return to help me attain my dream, just include a copy of *Teamworks!* and/or *Wishcraft* in the seminar price.)

You may wonder why I'm giving out these designs, teaching everyone to run my seminars, instead of running them all myself or franchising them. The answer is that I can't possibly run as many as people are asking for, and I'm not interested in the business of franchising seminars. Being in business isn't one of my goals. I try to limit myself to running ten seminars each year. The reason? I've already been successful in the seminar business. I'm ready to move on to another dream. My role model is I.F. Stone, the writer/publisher of *I.F. Stone's Weekly*, who retired and learned Greek at the age of seventy, and has just come out with a book on Socrates and Athens. I'm auditing classes in literature and trying to learn Latin these days.

But I believe so deeply in the value of these support groups I've worked so many years to design, that I want the work to go on. I would love for the world to be full of people who use my Success Teams to help others—and to benefit themselves. I'm hoping *Teamworks!* will spread the word for me, and that you'll be inspired to take the book and use it for your own purposes. In particular, I know from the volume of mail I've received year after year that there are many of you out there looking for a way to make a living doing something that feels important, that makes a contribution to the world by using the qualities in yourself you cherish most: concern, ingenuity, resourcefulness, and the desire to help others. You know who you are. I'm hoping you will take the *Teamworks!* seminars and run with them.

I've created the seminars in three lengths:

1. The *Teamworks!* short seminar fits the bare basics of goal-setting and team-building, plus an introduction to brainstorming and networking, into a time slot the size of a lunch hour or a dinner meeting. I usually run it in an hour and a half, but I've discovered that the essentials can be delivered in a lightning half-hour. It can also be extended to two hours or more, if you leave time afterward for people to mix and continue networking. Its length makes it an ideal kickoff for corporate Dream Teams (see p. 158), as well as a boon for busy people who can spare a lunch hour or an evening more easily than a whole day.

The short seminar is essentially a taste—an exciting demonstration of what can happen if people go after wishes and dreams with lots of other people helping them. Yet weekly lunchtime Success Team meetings, in company and school lunchrooms, that offer much more, grow out of it very naturally.

2. The *Teamworks!* full-day seminar takes six hours, and is a true training seminar. People don't go into it just to *think* about writing that book, buying that house, starting that business; they actually get their projects started. It's like attending a meeting of SmokEnders or Weight Watchers: they've laid down their money and committed themselves to begin.

Participants leave the full-day seminar with plans on paper, scheduled, with appointments and homework. And they are in a Success Team that they've been working with for hours, a team that's going to meet with them next week (and every week) to see how they're doing.

3. The *Teamworks!* course was originally run as a semester course in a school. That made it fourteen weeks long. Other schools ran it for twelve weeks. I ran it as an eight-week seminar in my living room. I know high school teachers and college counselors who've given it in their schools, and independents who've offered it for adults through the local Y, community college, learning exchange, or public library.

The first four meetings are devoted to team-building, goal-setting, and planning. After that, participants proceed in Success Teams with the career counselor's supervision. By the end of the course, most participants have made substantial progress toward their goals. Many teams continue to meet after the seminar ends.

Which version of the *Teamworks!* seminars should you offer? It depends on several factors: the time and resources available to you; how much money you want to charge; and how much commitment you want to ask for. It also depends on what your goal is in running the seminars—whether you want it to be one of your income-producing services, or primarily an advertisement for your career-counseling skills. I'll talk about the comparative advantages of each format in a minute. But first, I want to tell you what all three seminars have in common.

First of all, they are designed to require a minimum of talking by the leader and a maximum of interaction between participants. I designed them that way more by accident than anything else because that's what I was used to. My training is in encounter-group therapy. I like the action and energy that come from intense give-and-take between people. I'd never had the experience of teaching a class, so it never occurred to me to give lectures. Besides, I never knew what people needed until I asked them. My audiences always seemed happy, so I assumed that I was a pretty good speaker.

Then, one dark day, I discovered that I was wrong. I might be a pretty good designer of seminars, but a good speaker I was not.

I'd been asked to lecture on my support systems and Success Teams to a roomful of professionals who had been through the short seminar that morning. There was no point in demonstrating anything to them—they'd already experienced it. So I proceeded to explain the rationale behind each exercise, and to point out the ways I thought they could use the three seminars in their various fields.

They started dozing off within minutes! I was horrified. I got playful to entertain them, then outrageous to make them laugh—anything to hold back the soporific cloud that was descending over the room. Nothing worked. Somebody actually looked at his watch. Nothing like this had ever happened to me.

Finally, I said, ". . . and the last and very best reason to run the *Wishcraft/Teamworks!* seminars with your clientele is that it's the only way to teach Success Teams without putting your audience to sleep!" They began to stir, guiltily. I saw a few people smile. I tossed a question at them like a little firecracker: "How many of you got bored in the seminar this morning?" No hand went up. "How many of you are bored now?" They were a polite bunch, but some hands went halfway up. "I rest my case," I said, turned off the overhead projector, and bowed low. Startled by the suddenness of my ending, they started to laugh, and then to applaud. I prayed they thought I'd planned the whole thing, and I swore never again to stand up in front of a group of people and talk for an hour. My admiration for lecturers soared, and I went back to leading interactive seminars.

These three seminars almost run themselves. That is, the work that's done in each exercise is so involving for the participants that your job is reduced to little more than answering questions, asking for feedback (which builds the sense of possibility in the room and shows people who are feeling excited, emotional, or apprehensive that they are not alone), and describing the next exercise. Each exercise is designed to carry participants into the next one, so there's built-in direction. And the whole seminar has been orchestrated to take the audience to a high spot at the end.

It's a high spot because they will have learned one of the most heartening lessons any of us can learn: they can have what they want out of life, because the support they need really exists. It's available right there in the seminar room, all around them.

The seminars all break down into the same elements. (When I come to a segment—such as the networking game—that's described elsewhere in the book, I'll give you page numbers, so that you can easily find it.) All three seminars contain these basic units:

1. There is a warm-up speech in which I tell them what I am about to prove to them: that the wildest wish can be achieved without positive thinking, or pumping themselves up with words of courage, or self-discipline. To paraphrase the Beatles, you'll get by with a little help from your friends. I tell my audiences that I won't spend much time telling them how I'm going to prove this. I'll just be firing orders at them, and want them simply to do what I ask. I promise that they'll see at the end whether or not I was right, and get their chance to talk back.

2. The second section invites people to choose their wishes and tell them to someone else

First I remind them to aim high enough, not to be realistic or play it too safe. (I tell them to use the magic wand test: "If I could wave a magic wand and you'd have anything, what would it be?") I explain that if they protect themselves by picking something they don't really want, they'll be sorry halfway through the workshop. First of all, the skills they're about to learn won't work if they don't care about what they're aiming for. I'm giving them a great machine, but their desire is the power source that will make it fly. Secondly, so many wishes are going to start getting met in the room that they're going to need to change goals in midstream if they want to join in.

Virginia C., a painter and medical illustrator who was in one of my early seminars, remembers the impact of this segment: "Early in the seminar we all discovered how much we'd resisted allowing ourselves to think about absolutely magnificent, wonderful goals. We realized we'd been satisfied with crumbs too much of our lives, and weren't ever thinking in terms of the whole chocolate cake. We got through a lot of those inhibitions in the seminar. By the end of it we were ready to dream about delicious goals."

Then the participants form pairs with strangers, which I call focus dyads. This is a six-minute exercise. Two people work together; one asks the other the two basic *Teamworks!* questions—"What do you want?" and, on hearing the answer, "What's the problem?" The first listens while the other person talks. After three minutes, the seminar leader, acting as timekeeper, says, "Switch roles!" and the first listener gets his turn to speak.

The purpose of this exercise is to give everyone in the room the experience described in this book under "Tell a Friend" (p. 29): the rare experience of having someone listen to a personal dream with real interest and respect. The only difference is that in the seminar it's a stranger who's listening. That can be even more powerful than telling a friend, because there's no business as usual to clear away. New acquaintances know nothing about you but your heart's desire, and have no other purpose than to witness it. That makes their reactions believable, makes you start to hear yourself in a way that's new.

3. The third segment is feedback: reporting on the experience.

Participants need to hear the experiences of others to give a name to their own. Every feedback session raises the energy in the room (if you keep them brief—long feedback reports bring the energy down).

4. The fourth segment is the turning point of each seminar: a demonstration of what kind of resources are in the room—in other words, a large-group brainstorming (p. 59). Now the work begins that will change the direction of many lives. One or more people stand and tell their wishes to the room, so that the audience can start to produce ideas. Gears change—you can feel the whole group roll up their sleeves and get down to work. Connections are made, sparks fly, and the wealth of possibilities in the room reveals itself. After this, you have an audience full of believers. Now people can't wait to try the system on their own dreams.

5. The fifth element essential to any seminar is the experience of working in a Success Team. Two (or three, in the full-day) of the original pairs from the focus dyad exercise are combined into a group, and the goal of this grouping is to help each other with some personal project.

In a short seminar, this is called a focus team, and the team goal is simply to assist each member in preparing a clear statement of his or her wish and the obstacle to meeting it—a tightly focused statement to be written on a 3 × 5 card (see p. 64) for the networking game which will follow. The team has ten minutes, or two and a half minutes per person, to prepare each member so that her wish and obstacle are stated in the way that will generate the most responses. That person's buddy from the focus dyad stands by to help, because he is already knowledgeable about the goal.

For example, Sally, the schoolteacher you met at the beginning of this book, told her teammates, "I want a house by the sea, and the problem is money." They started firing questions: "Do you have to own the house, or would it be okay to rent or borrow it?" "By what sea, where?" "All year, or just over Christmas vacation?" "How much rent could you afford?" Sally's buddy, George, was able to help out by saying, "Remember, you told me you wanted it to be in a warm climate, with beautiful clear water. That sounds like Florida, or the Caribbean." They refined Sally's wish, and whittled it down, till Sally, who might have gone into the networking game asking for a quarter of a million dollars, had a card that said: *I want:* "To rent/borrow house on coast, San Diego or Florida, 2 months/ year," and *My obstacle:* "How to find house for under $300/mo?"

Participants find that having three other people help them prepare for the upcoming networking is unexpectedly heart-warming. It gives them a taste of being special, being groomed for something that matters. Granted, it's only a taste, not a meal, but the feelings are authentic, and very much like those they might feel if a coach were checking them out, slapping them on the shoulder, and sending them out to compete, like potential champs.

In the full-day seminar and the eight- to fourteen-week course, by contrast, the team goal is to begin working on each person's wish. In these seminars there is both the time and the need to weld a strong, working Success Team, so before putting them to work, I run two powerful team-building exercises that are described a little later in this book (see Chapter 10). In the full-day seminar and course, I also teach techniques for planning and scheduling, and for dealing with the resistance to action that often comes up. (At the end of this chapter I'll provide seminar maps to guide you through each seminar format step by step, repeating the page numbers in *Teamworks!* and in *Wishcraft* where all the source material can be found.)

6. The sixth essential element is a special version of networking. In the short and long seminars, that's done by playing the Networking Game (p. 64), in which everyone moves around the room, pairing up with as many people as possible for two minutes, to get ideas and information. In the semester course, outside guests are invited to the second-to-last meeting, where they sit in on the teams. It's a smash ending to the semester course. Friends, family, colleagues from work join in the final brainstorming, and become avid helpers in the process, although they've never seen anything like this before. Team members get a fresh and invigorating influx of new ideas, information and contacts. They will need the additional week to put the new information into their plans, and to get some re-assurance about the excitement ahead of them.

7. The seventh is a closure. In the short seminar, that's just me shouting over the din to say, "Was I right?" and hearing the answer of applause as I leave the stage. In the full-day seminar, closure is a go-around in which every person has a few moments to tell their reactions to the seminar, and what they're planning to do in the coming months.

You can sometimes have a go-around at the end of a lunch-time short seminar if you're working with a small group—it won't take too much time, and a small group has less trouble changing gears. But in the standard short seminar—one and a half hours, usually for a conference or membership meeting—it's impossible. This is a large group, and it's always out of control by the time the networking game is supposed to end—no one has any intention of doing anything I say. They will, as I've mentioned, answer my challenge with applause, but they don't turn and face me to say goodbye; they're too busy. (Incidentally, no chairperson has a chance for further an-nouncements. They have to be made earlier.) Needless to say, that's my favorite kind of ending for a seminar.

Closure for the course, in which you and the participants have been together for eight to twelve weeks, is an entirely different matter. Two issues are dealt with in the last meeting: a summary of each person's accomplishments and plans, and arrangements for the smooth transfer of team leadership from a professional coach—you—to the team itself. I'll talk about these issues under Team Troubleshooting below (p. 140).

Which seminar should you run?

The short seminar is the easiest to fill. It doesn't require too much from participants in terms of time, money, and commit-ment, yet it's exciting and fun to do. If you're doing this for the first time, or your main goal is to draw a large, enthusiastic audience and create an instant clientele for your career services, you should probably choose this one. You can go to a local organization and offer the workshop free or for a low fee, and run it at a regularly scheduled meeting of their membership. They'll do most of the job of promoting and filling the seminar.

The lunch-hour-length short seminar works well in a corporation. It requires only posting announcements, and usually draws fewer than thirty people, but it boosts company morale out of all proportion to its size (see Dream Teams, p. 158). You'll select this workshop to run if you presently work in a company and want a team for yourself, or as a professional trainer if you want to offer a program to corporations that's easy for them to accept because it requires so little time and money.

Do you want to get your organization working hard on their plans right away? Or would you like to bring in a sizable fee by giving seminars? In that case, the full-day seminar may be best. The real construction begins immediately. And you can charge a higher fee for delivering a full day of training. However, without a ready-made membership to work with, filling a full-day seminar is hard work. For many people, setting aside a day, and the money, to attend a full-day training seminar is a major commitment. The excitement is just as great as in the short seminar—maybe even more so—but it's tempered by the serious business of problem-solving and planning, and by the sobering (if also thrilling) experience of taking real steps. So you'll have to do more publicizing, advertising, organizing—and sometimes hand-holding, to fill it. (Turn to Create-an-Event Team, p. 194 below, for stories of how some enterprising women in Illinois put together their own little seed team to produce a full-day seminar.) Many independent career counselors prefer to start with the short seminar, and then run the full-day seminar a few months later, once the word has gotten out. Social workers and others working with agencies often begin with the full-day seminar.

The eight- to fourteen-week course will suit you if you typically work with a semester format, or if you enjoy extended involvement with people, and like guiding their actual progress. The course can either be self-contained and end after the semester, or it can be a format for launching ongoing Success Teams. Susan Hadley, a career counselor and high school teacher in Nyack, New York, runs an eight-week course for adults at her public library. There are often ten to fifteen participants in a course. "I've found that when the eight sessions are over, they really need ongoing support, or they go off and kind of fall on their noses," says Susan. Her way of providing support is to invite graduates to meet once a month at her house for a networking session (see p. 64 for the format). As an alternative, you can pair participants off and have them look out for each other, using the buddy system (see p. 182), or divide the group into Success Teams that will keep meeting on their own.

Here's a close-up look at an actual *Teamworks!* short seminar.

When I first was asked to do the short seminar in *a half hour*, I was completely taken aback. I couldn't imagine how people would react to being raced through this already speedy workshop. I walked into the conference room of a large city agency, where about fifteen unsuspecting people were sitting around a table, opening brown bags and starting to eat sandwiches. They'd been to such programs before, and expected a peaceful, informative lecture. I knew I was going to ruin their lunch anyway, so I got right into it.

I said, "I'm going to show you a magic trick." That was my entire opening speech. I gave jet instructions: "Pair off and tell each other your deepest wish, the thing you want most for yourself [focus dyad]. We're going to get it for you today. You have three minutes each." I clicked an imaginary stopwatch with my thumb and said, "Go!"

The sandwiches hit the table. Startled and more than a little confused, they paired off and tried to remember their deepest wishes. After six minutes I stopped them, asked for reports [feedback] and found out what some of their wishes were. I selected one for the whole group to work on [demonstration brainstorming]: a woman wanted to pursue painting, but she had too many responsibilities and not enough time.

Within minutes, the group had given her a dozen ways to find time. Then they discovered the real problem: she felt selfish taking the time from her other obligations, because she might not be a great painter. After all, only a great painter has the right to be so selfish, right? At that point, a woman wrote something on a piece of paper and leaned over the table to hand it to her. "This is a collective of women painters who work and put on shows together for that very reason," she said. "Call them."

Now the group was excited and in the mood to play. They looked eagerly to me for the next instructions. I put them into teams of three (I usually have at least four in each team, but the less time you have, the smaller the team you must create). I instructed them to briefly hammer out for each person details of how to proceed to achieve their goals (they got four minutes each!). [This combined the team experience—the whole team helping one member build a plan—and networking elements, exchanging ideas, contacts, and information.] By now the food was in a chaos of waxed paper and cola cans in the center of the table and everyone was writing furiously on yellow pads. They were looking up, firing questions, writing again. There were sudden bursts of laughter; one man leaned back in his chair with his hands to his head saying "All right! All right!"; the painter put her cheek on the table, let her arms fall to the floor, and stared at me with disbelief in the middle of the din. I couldn't help laughing.

After twelve minutes I stopped them. "All right, you have fifteen seconds each to tell me what has happened to each of you and what you're going to do next" [closure/go-around].

The first woman who spoke had come in late. She said, "Oh, sure. Who's going to help you in this world? Everyone has their own problems. I haven't got the money to pay for the help I need." I looked at the group with a grin. "Honest, she's not a ringer. I didn't ask her to say that." But they were already answering her.

"We'll help each other!"

"Come on *time* next week, Helen!"

"*You're* going to help *me*, Helen!"

That was a wonderful seminar. Who made it wonderful? It wasn't me. They did it all. They contributed the imagination, the ingenuity, and the emotion.

And they did it in a half hour.

The only difference between the seminar I've just described and the standard short seminar is that I take a little additional time with each segment and make the small team a four-member focus team, with its goal to give each member a clear wish statement and put it on a 3 × 5 card to use in the networking game, which I add at the end. The flexibility of the format is such that the seminar adapts well to all sorts of changes, as long as all the basic elements are there.

I left handwritten instructions with this half-hour workshop group on how to proceed with their weekly team meetings. These days I hand out *Teamworks!* instead.

Now for the maps of the seminars. These will give you the page numbers in *Teamworks!* and the chapters in *Wishcraft* in which exercises are described in detail.

MAP: THE *TEAMWORKS!* LONG SEMINAR (6 HOURS)

In this format, my opening speech is longer, more leisurely, and designed to put participants at ease by making them laugh and loosen up. I also try to make them realize that the standards here are very different from any other seminar they've been to. No self-improvement, no positive attitudes required. I want to create a sense of relief. To do that I usually explain to them what a hopeless case I am (it's all true) and how they're going to learn goal achievement skills that work for even hopeless cases. For your opening speech, say what you wish or follow my example: read the first chapters of this book to remind yourself. Remember, I'm the person who jogged only once.

I don't speed them through exercises as I do in the lunchtime seminar, because I know that pace can't be kept up for a full day. In fact, I orchestrate the long seminar to move slowly in the morning (in clock terms, at least—so much happens that it feels jam-packed with action), to speed up at lunch, settle in to hard work in the early afternoon, and climax with speeded-up, high-energy action, ending at 4:00. I don't want them to leave at 4:00, and after the networking game, they don't want to. I stick around too, and wander through the crowd talking to people.

In my opening speech I let them know what the schedule is: we'll be doing team-building exercises for the next half hour, then working in teams and doing brainstorming until lunch. At lunch they'll practice networking. They'll learn flow charts and planning techniques after lunch. At 4:00 we'll break for wine and cheese, and socialize for an hour.

The map:

Morning: 3 hours
—Opening speech
—Team-building exercises, the color exercise and assets feedback (p. 108)
   —ask for feedback
—Teamwork: refining the goal, starting to find solutions
—Demonstration brainstorming (pp. 33 and 59)

Lunch: 1½ hours, on site
—Networking
(I give them guidelines for how they are to proceed: "Go to lunch, practice networking like crazy, come back with twenty ideas and names on your pad.")

Afternoon: 2½hours
—Ask for feedback on networking
(This is a way of pulling the room back together: "Did anyone get any interesting ideas or information at lunch?" I don't say "What happened at lunch?" because I only want to hear the success stories. They show what is possible, and in what direction the seminar is heading. Hearing about exciting connections made at lunch gives the people who were unable to network an important lesson: they see the potential that they didn't use, and they know that the seminar is half over. After this they start working with real energy for the rest of the day.)

—Hard Times
At some point, usually about now, the morning's high begins to give way to mild panic and a drop in energy. Paradoxically, it's because the prospect of actually getting those goals is starting to look very real. The games are starting to give way to memories of old disappointments. Fear starts to enter the picture: fear of success and change, or stage fright. The best way to deal with fear is to acknowledge and release it in a special kind of gripe session—one which starts out heavy and quickly turns funny. I call it a Hard Times session. I ask for a show of hands from people who've been having doubts or hesitant feelings, and call on them to stand up and make some rip-

roaring negative statements while the rest of the group cheers and applauds and tries to top the speaker with more negative statements. Some sample complaints from a real seminar:

—"This isn't the right goal."

—"I'd better stay where I am—something bad might happen."

—"I'm too old, and I should accept that it's too late."

—"It was a dumb idea to begin with."

—"It can't be done."

—"I will be ridiculed because I am *ridiculous*."

—"If I make it, I'll find myself alone at the top."

Hard times is always a great relief. It frees up the energy and motivates everybody to go on. For more guidance: p. 74 above, pp. 131 and 147 below, and *Wishcraft*, Chapter 5.

—Planning backward (p. 68), which is the same as Flow-Charting and Scheduling (*Wishcraft*, Chapters 6 and 8). This means taking ideas from the teamwork, brainstorming, and networking sections, and working them down to first steps, entering them in a calendar.

—Networking game (p. 64)

—Coffee and cookies, or wine and cheese

MAP: THE *TEAMWORKS!* COURSE

This course can be run over a period of eight to fourteen weeks. The first three or four meetings are always the same and are described on the next page. The rest are regular Success Team meetings, largely run by team members themselves, with the leader available but unobtrusive.

In fact, when running the course for adults, I announce after the fourth or fifth meeting (the first regular Success Team meeting) that I'm going to be absent for a certain number of meetings—and I won't tell them in advance which ones. When I ran the course over fourteen weeks, I was deliberately absent six times (after the fourth meeting). If you run the course for eight weeks, you might only want to be absent once or twice.

This places the responsibility where it belongs—on the team members. At first they flounder without a leader, but they soon get their footing and do very well on their own. In a classroom or afterschool format with high school students, the teacher/ leader might not choose to be absent at all. (See the section addressed to school guidance counselors on p. 163.)

The map:

—First session: Team-building exercises: the Color Exercise and Assets Feedback (for the teacher: prepare by reading Chapter 12)
　　—Students' homework for next week:
　　—Think about what you want to set as your goal.
　　—Read: The goalsearch questions (p. 35) ("What do you do like breathing," "What did you love to do as a child," etc.) and *Wishcraft*, Chapter 3: Stylesearch and Chapter 4: Goalsearch
　　—Respond to your favorite questions(s) or do your favorite exercise(s) in writing.

—Second session: Goalsearch and goalsetting (for the teacher: prepare by reading Chapter 11 and *Wishcraft*, Chapter 4: Goalsearch)
Students ask each other the goalsearch questions and share any written responses they've brought in. The class (or smaller sub-teams within a large class) helps each member: 1) set a goal that embodies what she or he loves; 2) clearly define the obstacles to it.
　　—Students' homework for next week: p. 68 on Planning; *Wishcraft*, Chapter 6: Brainstorming and Chapter 8: Working with Time

—Third session: Planning, flow-charting, scheduling (for the teacher: prepare by reading pp. 33 and 59, on brainstorming; p. 68, on planning; *Wishcraft*, Chapters 6 and 8; and preview *Wishcraft*, Chapters 5 and 9, on negativity and fear)
Students take turns having the whole group brainstorm their individual goals and obstacles.
(If the group is large, do a demonstration brainstorming

for three or four people, then divide the class into smaller teams to continue brainstorming.) The teacher then chooses a volunteer and demonstrates planning backward to first steps. Each student designs an action path from the ideas she or he has gotten in brainstorming. By the end of this session, each student will have first steps scheduled for the coming week.

The teacher prepares students for the possibility that they may experience negativity or apprehension (as well as excitement) as they begin to move. Class members are encouraged to call each other during the week.

—Students' homework for next week:

    —Do your first steps and be ready to report on them!

    —Read *Wishcraft*, Chapter 5: Hard Times and Chapter 9: Winning Through Timidation

    —Start an Actions and Feelings Journal ("What I did/ How I felt") from *Wishcraft*, p. 105

—Fourth session (and all subsequent sessions until the last two): Regular Success Team meeting (for the teacher: prepare by reading Chapters 12 and 13: How to Run a Success Team: The Third and All Subsequent Meetings, p. 125, and Team Troubleshooting, p. 136)

    —Homework from now on:

    —Taking steps toward your goal, and supporting your teammates!

—Next-to-last meeting: Invite guests for networking (see large group brainstorming, p. 59)

—Last meeting: Each team member tells accomplishments and plans (p. 88), farewell party, and transition to independent teams (teacher should be familiar with team troubleshooting, p. 136 below)

The next chapter will show you how to get a team together on your own, without going through a *Wishcraft/Teamworks!* seminar.

9...

Finding Your Team, Part 2: On Your Own

If you have a dream, and you want support, you can create your own Success Team from scratch. Unlike people who get their teams through a seminar, you can choose your own teammates. You might consider joining up with another person who wants a Success Team. The two of you can get the rest of the team together more easily than you can alone.

The following guidelines for finding your team have been drawn from talks with team veterans all over the country.

—How many people are best for a team?

The most successful, long-lasting Success Teams have four or five members. (Some of the special variations on a team discussed later have more or fewer, for good reasons, but here we're talking about the basic, all-purpose Success Team.) More than six people makes meetings too long. Three or fewer means that meetings will be vulnerable to cancellation when someone can't come.

However: to find those four or five core people who are committed to the team, you usually have to start with more. Team veterans' experience suggests strongly that you should start with six to eight people. Some may drop out because of time pressures, or become successful and relocate. Some teams prefer to start with four or five and replace anyone who drops out.

Many teams have successfully integrated a latecomer (on p. 139 I'll tell you how).

—Should teams be made up of friends, acquaintances, or strangers?

These are the three populations from which you might decide to choose your teammates. Each has advantages and drawbacks:

Close friends are, in some ways, the easiest to approach with a proposal like, "Let's start a Success Team!" "The advantage of friends for me was the ability to share personal feelings and ambitions comfortably," says Ronda H. of Skokie, Illinois, who formed a *Wishcraft* group with two friends. But the familiarity of friends is also their drawback. Friendships have habits built into them—rhythms and rituals of behavior, ways of seeing each other—and it can be hard to teach an old relationship new tricks. Friends may feel silly holding a business meeting with strict time limits, and may be especially apt to lapse into socializing or commiserating during the business meeting, which is death to a Success Team (see p. 136).

Some people also feel uncomfortable revealing new facets of themselves to old friends. "I knew this lawyer, and I thought he would be very good in the team, but I was a little hesitant about letting in a good friend while I was saying all these things I'd like to do," says Marcia J., an airline employee with an ambition to act. "I can tell strangers, but I'm more afraid of friends' judgments. And I think they can be reluctant to see you change, because they've had you pegged since you were in third grade." Others report being comfortable opening up to friends. You know best what's right for you.

Acquaintances—from work, from your school or church or health club, neighbors, friends of friends—are, in many ways, the best group of people to draw your team from. You don't share established habits or emotional entanglements; there's a kind of refreshing objectivity to your relationship, and the possibilities are wide open. But you usually do know enough about acquaintances to be able to answer some questions that help identify good teammates:

—First, are these acquaintances motivated toward action and life change? (They don't have to be super hot-shot go-getters. They do have to be ready to move.)

"I can tell you what made our team work so well," says painter and medical illustrator Virginia C. "Every person in it was motivated. We didn't all know what we wanted to do, or exactly how we were going to do it, but we all knew we wanted to stop being stuck, and to go on and be successful in some way."

Springfield, Illinois, career coach Jane Shuman started out in a team that didn't work. "The bottom line was that two of the four people in the group were looking for an emotional support group, rather than a Success Team, which is very action-oriented. These two women weren't highly motivated toward change or toward meeting goals. So the other woman and I, who had been the mainstay, had a meeting ourselves, and we decided that we really did want a Success Team, and that we were going to re-create one and more carefully select the people whom we invited to belong." Both of the women they asked to join the new team were acquaintances: a hospital administrator working on her master's degree, and a dancer and world traveler. Jane describes them both as goal-oriented, action-oriented, and creative. The new team has flourished, and after two years it's still going strong.

—Second, are these acquaintances in transition?

"Another woman and I started the group together," says Julie Dunleavy, an Albuquerque, New Mexico counselor who leads *Wishcraft* groups and teaches at Webster University. "We both knew a lot of people who were either trying to figure out what they wanted to do, or were trying to make a career change. And since they'd been mentioning it to us in conversation, we called all these people up and said, 'Would you like to join us?' We thought it would be useful to them. We all already knew each other, but we weren't close friends at the time. Good friendships developed out of it."

Strangers have the advantage of freshness and surprise. If you want to meet new people—if you just moved to a new town, or become single, or you want to add some new people to the old cast of characters, strangers are what you want. One way to find new people is by advertising. Try these places:

—Classified ads in local newspapers. Julie Dunleavy told us that several people have advertised in the Albuquerque paper for people wanting to join *Wishcraft* working groups. Alternative papers like the *Boston Phoenix* and the *Chicago Reader* have classified-ad sections. Ads can say, "Have you read *Wishcraft* or *Teamworks*? Want to join a new Success Team? Call Sara at 555-1234."
—Community bulletin boards—in the company lunchroom, the laundromat, the library, the mall, the student union.
—Bookstores. Ask your local bookstore to let you post a notice in their window or on their bulletin board. They're usually delighted—after all, you're advertising one of their books.

Of course, the darker side of surprise is risk; when you advertise for strangers, you're fishing in the unknown. You will want to screen potential teammates—to make sure you don't enlist anyone with noticeably severe psychological problems (a personal Success Team is not equipped to handle such problems).

Jeannie Schatzki, a trainer and career counselor in Basking Ridge, New Jersey, puts teams together in New York. Whenever people call me asking to be put in a team, I give their names to Jeannie. Here's how she screens them: "I talk to everybody first for at least ten minutes on the phone. I ask them where they heard about teams, what they're doing now, and what they'd like from the team. If they sound like congenial people, sane, and not obnoxious, basically that's all. I occasionally screen out people who talk constantly, who I feel would take over the group."

When having a first team meeting with strangers, it's a good idea to meet in a restaurant or other public place.

—Similarity or diversity?

Variety is the spice of most Success Teams. There are special kinds of teams for people who are all in the same boat (The Job Club, p. 192; Kick-the-Habit Clubs, p. 198; Guilds, p. 201; Mentor-Apprentice Teams, p. 208). Check them out to see if they fit your situation. But most people flourish in a team with a wide spectrum of goals and resources. For one thing, it's fascinating and refreshing to be in touch with different kinds of people. Ronda H. puts her finger on the chief drawback of a too-homogeneous team: "The problem with our group, I felt, was we were too much alike (married, young children, not working, two teachers, two medical residents' wives), therefore limiting the nature of suggestions and alternatives."

There are, of course, situations where you have a narrow range of people to choose your team from: in retirement communities and company towns, for example, or on military bases. In that case, you can bring variety in by remembering that the deeper you delve, the more different people are. (The first Team-Building exercise in Chapter 10—Pick a Color—will help you do the delving.) You and your teammates may have similar worldly resources and limitations, but on the level of imagination and talent, your minds probably work very differently: one person is visual, another is logical, a third grasps the world through emotion and music. There's diversity in every team, whether it's diversity of professional fields or just of cognitive styles. Emphasize the ways that you differ, and you'll have more resources to bring to bear on problem-solving.

The variety in these successful teams was a major contributing factor in their success:

Derek C., Somerville, Massachusetts: "There are, at the moment, two women and two men. There were three women. We range in age from early thirties to middle fifties. We have a man who's self-employed in the construction industry. I teach at MIT, and I'm an actor and director. We have a woman who works as a freelance arts consultant, another woman who works as a physical therapist in a hospital, and the one who has left the group to fulfill a dream and a challenge is a teacher."

Arlene S., Boston, Massachusetts: "There are four of us: a thirty-six-year-old woman advertising director; a thirty-six-year-old man in software sales; an artist, wife, and mother in her late forties; and a man in his sixties who's a retail furniture executive. We just celebrated our first anniversary."

Virginia C., Brooklyn, New York: "I was a painter, and I had done some medical illustration, and I was going to have to make up my mind which way to go. It looked as if medical illustration would be it, because I was good at it, and I was coming out of a divorce with two children to support. There was a woman who had been an actress and was solidifying a new career as a fund-raiser for the arts and health care. There was a woman who had been working in the hospital system with mentally retarded children, and she was suffering burnout. She wanted to do something completely different, and she didn't know what, but she wanted to make a lot of money. There was a woman who was a writer and a singer. And then there was a graphic artist."

Marcia J., New York City: "I work for an airline, but I'm looking to make a change to something in the arts. Another woman in our team was a single mother, a brilliant math and computer whiz who'd lost her teaching job. She was really floundering—she wanted to get out of the city but had no idea where she was going to go. Another teammate was a holistic healer. The fourth woman was in public relations. She had just moved to New York from California, and she was trying to land her dream job at a public-TV station."

In the pages to come, you'll read some of the wonderful success stories that came out of these teams, and you'll see how variety multiplies serendipity—the sheer number of surprising ways that teammates can help each other. Just one cautionary note, from Jeannie Schatzki, on putting different kinds of people together in teams: "The one kind of conflict that sometimes comes up is between high-powered people, who mostly want business networking, and gifted underachievers, who need more support. The people who are moving faster get impatient with the ones who aren't—'Just go *do* it! What's the big deal?'—and the ones who aren't get a little bit intimidated by the ones who are."

I really think that impatient fast-trackers are paying too little attention to their feelings, and overcautious slow-trackers are paying too much attention to theirs. In principle, they could help each other, and I've seen it happen. Still, a fast-tracker in a support team is usually looking for contacts and strategies only, and a slow-tracker is looking for confidence. If that's the case, they can cause each other real discomfort. Take that into consideration when you're selecting teammates.

A good team will usually have at least one natural-born resource person in it—the kind who's always opening her address book and saying, "Oh, I know somebody in computers! I know how you can find a patent lawyer. Here's somebody you can talk to about motorcycles!" If you find someone like that, you're in luck. They keep things exciting and are greatly valued by the other members. Just be sure that person gets as much help as she gives.

—Women, men, or both?

As I mentioned when I was talking about the *Teamworks!* seminars, until now the majority of people in Success Teams have been women. "The handful of men we've had have worked out very well, but there haven't been that many," says Jeannie Schatzki. "I think it's the whole societal thing that men just don't do that—go in and admit that they don't know what they're doing and they need help."

But all this is changing. Some men like Success Teams. They admit that they like getting and giving support. Some of them emphasize the practicality, others the intimacy. "The sheer fact of putting things down on paper and time-lining them and setting checkpoints for yourself, and the monitoring mechanism of the group meeting to say, 'How are you doing and what can we do to help?,' enhances the likelihood of accomplishment," said Boston banker David E., who was the only regularly attending male on his team. "I was in the process of changing jobs within the company where I'd been for nine years, when an opportunity came along that had all the ele-

ments of what I was looking for in terms of career advance-
ment—except that it was with another institution. I found that
I was probably much more predisposed to make that change
than I would have been without the support of the group. I
sat there with what has turned out to be a really fine opportunity, and I was sort of being overly deliberative about it, and
I was sharing these thoughts with the people in the group, and
they kept saying, 'What are you waiting for? Isn't this what
you're looking for? Hey, David—*go* for it!' It was really effective
and useful and helpful."

David belonged to an action-oriented team of mostly women.
Actor/director Derek C.'s team, equally balanced by male and
female members, chose a different style—a balance of action
and introspection. "Even though the team tends to be goal-
oriented, in the process you can't help but reveal a lot about
your inner life, and the kinds of issues and problems that are
stopping you from doing what you feel you might be doing,"
says Derek. "And so without actually being a form of therapy,
it becomes a kind of cleansing or healing process, in which all
these people get to know and trust each other in very intimate
and direct ways. It really has been an exceptionally rewarding
experience for all of us."

So, although some men resist the idea of a mutual helping
group, the ones who don't make excellent team members.

On the other hand, there's still a case to be made for the
good old all-woman team.

"One of the things that I think is neat about women is that
the personal and the professional always intertwine," says Den-
ver, Colorado, psychotherapist Lucy F., whose four-woman
team has been meeting for over a year. "So we can be serious
about our professional goals, but then if something comes up
—we need to spend a month getting our house uncluttered,
because the closets are driving us crazy—*that* becomes the goal."
As you read Lucy's amazing account of all the things she and
her teammates do for each other, consider whether you'd like
to have a team like this—and whether a team including men
could do it.

"The woman who works for the local TV station worked for
a while on getting into the old boys' network that was domi-
nating the news department. She wasn't getting the stories,

the tips, and the leads. So we looked at strategies for making her stronger professionally, more visible, being able to create ties to the people who had the power to make the stories break. We did the brainstorming, and then gave her reinforcement as she came back each week saying, 'I did this and it worked, and I did that and it didn't work.' And we'd brainstorm why it didn't work, and so forth. She's also working toward a master's degree in economic journalism, and she had kind of put that on the shelf for a while, so she started working on her thesis again, which was the point where she'd been stuck. We worked on everything from scheduling to getting her writing going and having her bring something to each meeting for us to read.

"We also planned her wedding. Two women in the group ended up getting married during the last year, and we handled the details of ordering the flowers and the dresses and all that. One of the women needed to talk with her new husband about financial planning in their relationship—working out who controls the money and how decisions get made—and we helped her set goals for sitting down and talking with him, setting up new budgets, and so on.

"Another woman has been having some job unhappiness, and probably will end up leaving the career she's in now. She's a fund-raiser for a regional museum, and she's languishing in this job that has her working with computers all by herself, when she's really a people person. So we encouraged her to find a project *in* the job that connected with something central in her. She ended up planning a big fund-raiser called *The Great Museum Mystery*, where she got someone to write a murder mystery, and she became the producer and director. She got people in the community to play the parts of the murderer and so on, and it took place in the museum, and people paid $25 or $50 and had to come and spend the evening witnessing the murder and solving the crime and eating and having a good time. This project used all of her wonderful skills—her organizing ability, her way of involving people, her playfulness, her gift for food—and it was a huge success.

"Once that was over, she was back sitting alone at her computer again. So we've spent some time working out a stress-management program for her—we got her involved in taking weaving classes. Also, she's married to a financial analyst and he knew all about investments and mutual funds, and she didn't know a thing. So one of her initial goals was to develop a small investment program of her own, to gain some sense of personal control over her finances within their marriage. We brainstormed that, and she ended up taking a six-week class in investments, and having coffee meetings with some people who were into mutual funds, who could explain and work with her.

"Another woman got married early in the year—we planned her wedding—and she just had a baby. And I am about to deliver my first baby, and I'm forty-three years old. So the support of the team was very important to me. There were decisions to make. I'm a take-charge person. Do I just go through the normal routine that women go through when they go to the hospital and give birth, or do I try to have more control over the process? The other woman was pregnant three months ahead of me, so we've ended up spending much of the year making it our project to have these babies.

"We've gone to natural-childbirth classes together. We have made a search together to find obstetricians who were supportive of natural childbirth and letting us have some say in how the babies were delivered. We both had to take a lot of responsibility for our diet—and for exercise, which I absolutely hate. So for a while my Success Team was walking with me, three times a week! I felt rather silly doing that, but I remembered your example of two people getting through a Ph.D. program—one calling the other up every morning and saying, 'I'm coming over to sit at your kitchen table with you while you write for two hours.' So the team got me through the exercise part of it.

"The team has also been working with me on plans for phasing out of my full-time job and launching my private practice in career counseling. I've been on the counseling staff at a university for seventeen years, and I had gotten into a maintenance rather than a creative role in that job. I'm a creative person, so I was really kind of languishing. The team has been helping me draw up business plans and marketing strategies for my practice. I'm now working in my job half-time, and I have about twenty-five private clients. After the baby is born,

I'll probably go on my own full-time. *Wishcraft* and my team have given me the courage to do what I want to do, and I'm doing well and loving it."

Lucy's all-woman team has spun off an all-male brother team. "Our husbands see us going away every other Sunday for our meetings, and coming back with sheets of things to do that we paste on the refrigerator door—and they feel left out! One of them is an artist who goes through great periods of not producing, and his wife said, 'If you really want a Success Team, I'll help you do it.' So he got together three buddies, and she's training them in the Success Team techniques. They've been meeting now for six weeks."

There's no foolproof recipe for a good team. That mysterious thing called chemistry is one of the ingredients that determine whether a team works well and how long it keeps on meeting. But the guidelines I've just given you are designed to maximize your chances of picking good teammates the first time around. (And if your first team shipwrecks, all you have to do is grab the fellow survivor you like best, go out together and recruit some others.)

Okay—find four to eight promising people, and I'll tell you everything you need to know to turn them into a team: two team-building exercises and—the rules. Because the other ingredient that makes teams work and keep on working isn't mysterious at all. There are a few basic, unbreakable rules at the heart of any Success Team's success. They are very simple, but the best chemistry in the world won't work without them. With them, even so-so chemistry can often be alchemized into a great team.

10...

How to Run a Success Team, the First Meeting: Team-Building

You've got a group of people together for your first team meeting. They're sitting around your living room, looking at each other. Some of them may know each other; some don't. How do you get this slightly stiff social gathering to melt and flow into a working team? Do you all speak in turn, introduce yourselves, and then start talking about goals? If you do, some people may feel uncomfortable. The room is still too chilly.

To become a team you need a real room-warmer, a shortcut to knowing the best of each other. For that, you run the following two team-building exercises. These exercises are the fastest way of making a group into a team that I ever saw. Ideally, you should run them right at the start of the first meeting, before anyone has much time to exchange vital statistics. There's a very good reason for doing that, and I'll tell you what it is.

In a Success Team, people are not valued for status, accomplishments, or profession. Each of you is here to give a voice to your original self—the core of talent, style, and passion that makes you who you are. That's the most vulnerable, but most powerful, part of everyone, and it is normally the best protected. We almost never get to know that side of a stranger, and we don't always get to know that side of a friend. By running the team-building exercises at your team's beginning, the strangers in the group will get a unique introduction to each other, and those who are already friends or acquaintances will gain surprising new insights. These two exercises also establish the right climate for teamwork: the feel of an ideal family that cherishes the unique creative spark in each of you.

Note: If a career counselor is on hand to help launch your team, she or he will facilitate these exercises. If you're starting up on your own, one person should take charge of giving the instructions and keeping time. It's usually either the person who got the team together or the person whose house the first meeting is at (they may be one and the same). The question of who, if anyone, should lead your team over time is discussed in depth on pp. 140–43 (rotating leadership wins hands down). But, remember, the timekeeper engages in the exercises just as the other members do.

TEAM-BUILDING EXERCISE 1: PICK A COLOR

I discovered this exercise years ago, when I attended an affective education workshop for elementary-school teachers in Amherst, Massachusetts, given by Jack Canfield. Jack put us through this exercise with the intention of showing us how to teach it to children. I was in the workshop by chance, and had no particular interest in meeting a roomful of elementary-school teachers ten years younger than I was. I didn't see how we had any concerns in common, and I assumed that they were all pretty much alike—a self-selected, homogeneous group.

We sat in groups of seven or eight, and were instructed to pick a color we liked. Each of us was asked to tell what color we were, and what characteristics we had as that color. One after the other, everyone spoke. "I am green. I'm like a forest, dark and cool and quiet, with light falling through in tiny pieces, like little jokes," said one shy young man. I sat up and started paying attention. "I'm blue, like a late evening sky, wide and clear and distant and intelligent," said a small plump woman.

That was over fifteen years ago, and I'll never forget one of those people. I saw into strangers in a way we're rarely allowed to, and I found every one of them to be extraordinarily rich and amazingly different from each other. My mind raced around at the potential I saw: "We should all go into business together, we should help that one become a poet . . . et cetera."

I was so impressed with the results of this exercise that I got Jack's permission to use it in my first seminars, and subsequently in *Wishcraft*. It's child's play—and for just that reason, it's both difficult and delightful for adults. It's a powerful first step in building a team.

> —Each of you picks a color that you like. It can be a color in your mind's eye, one that you're wearing, or one you see in the room.
> —Don't worry if everyone in the room picks blue. You'll all see the color differently.
> —Take turns speaking. Each of you takes up to one minute (many of you will be through in fifteen or twenty seconds) to speak, in the first person, *for* your color. You should not say, "I like blue because . . ." You *are* blue, describing itself. You can be serious or poetic—or funny. "I am beige. Everyone needs me." "I'm fuchsia, and if you clash with me, that's *your* problem!"

That's the first of the two team-builders. It's the lowest-risk get-to-know-each-other exercise that I know of. I'm not comfortable with high-risk ones where you're expected to cry and talk about your personal relationships in front of strangers. But even this exercise is tougher than it looks. It's embarrassing to make "I" statements, even if they're supposed to be about a color. Is that because we're really talking about ourselves?

Not necessarily. I might pick pearl gray and say, "I am gray. I am cool and distant and elegant and dreamy," and I don't think there's a word in there that's true of me: I'm hot, close up, rumpled, and noisy! But this exercise would tell why I love that color: it might reveal a quality that I long for, like the wishes and dreams I should be working toward. (Will I grow up to be a cool, distant, elegant, and dreamy old lady?)

This exercise reveals how you think and feel and what you value—your personal taste, your style. And personal style is not trivial. It may even be the one uncompromised statement of your identity. You don't always get to pick the career you want; you don't always get to work or live where you want; you certainly don't get to act the way you want—but your style is all your own. And so most of us use personal style as a defiant, shorthand declaration of our qualities and gifts.

It's the creative core of each other that you meet when you launch your team with Pick a Color—not who's rich and who's poor, who's shy or pretty or witty, and all the other ways we usually assess a roomful of strangers to figure out how we fit in. Meeting new people can be a competitive or threatening situation. But this exercise makes an end run around the tendency to invidious comparison, and starts your team off on the basis of variety, not competition. No one feels competitive about someone else's color. That's because, while you might be able to compare your singing voice or math ability to mine, you can't compare my blue to your orange, or even my blue to your blue. All you can do is notice how different they are, how the contrast—subtle or strong—brings out each color's uniqueness.

The next exercise is harder—and even more amazing.

TEAM-BUILDING EXERCISE 2: ASSETS FEEDBACK (OR: PRAISE BEHIND YOUR BACK)

This is my favorite exercise ever. I don't say that just because I invented it. I say it because I've seen what it does to people.

My reasons for coming up with this exercise in 1975 seemed simple enough: I had always wanted to hear people saying nice things about me behind my back. I didn't need constructive criticism. I was trained in confrontation therapy. There wasn't a bad thing you could say about me that I hadn't heard before, at top volume. I hated criticism, but I was used to it; I knew how to process it. And I don't think I improved because of it; I just learned to behave myself. But there were times when people would say something complimentary and very precise about me, and it would invariably shock me, hit me with a kind of insight I was unaccustomed to. I didn't completely understand why, but I knew that hearing those good things—things that both surprised me and that I recognized as true—opened me up, made me feel something new, made me trust something inside myself, and did change me. So I decided that it would be a good idea for people to have that experience when they were about to launch a new, risky phase in their lives.

I also remembered that after I'd hear one of those powerful, good things about myself, I wanted to be alone to think about it. I didn't want to thank anybody, or be looked at. So it seemed perfect to *overhear* praise, hear it behind my back, as though no one knew I was listening. That would provide the privacy to allow me to really feel the impact. And that's why I designed Assets Feedback (also known, more accurately and awkwardly, as Chairback Feedback and Praise Behind Your Back). I gave it a few trial runs in my own pilot team, and it worked beautifully, so I incorporated it into the first Success Teams seminar.

In that seminar, in September 1976, after I'd given the instructions, and fifty people in groups of five or six were engaged in this exercise, I strolled around the room, and for the first time I saw the faces of people whose backs were turned to the group, who were hearing themselves being praised. They were writing sometimes, other times just looking out into the room. It's a look I've never seen anywhere else. Almost to a person they were soft, flushed, and completely unselfconscious. I would bend down and look right in their faces, and although they'd see me, they would only smile absentmindedly and continue listening and writing down what was being said behind them. Often they'd have tears in their eyes, or be shaking their heads and laughing—or both at the same time. Angry people became soft, vulnerable people became triumphant, shy people laughed out loud. I've never seen anything like it.

I've used that exercise more than a hundred times now, and it's never been different. Run immediately after Pick a Color it is an extraordinarily powerful way to create trust and generosity in a group of strangers.

I believe these two exercises could make a Success Team out of marble statues in a museum. Here are the instructions:

—Bring your chairs into a close circle.
—Have one person turn his back, so he can't see the others

but can hear them. The turned chair is often called the hot seat, very aptly, as you'll see. He should have a pencil and paper ready.

The first person to turn his back should be the most outspoken or extroverted. Finding his assets will be easy, and talking to each other about him will subtly reveal everyone else's character. After that the order doesn't matter.

—For about two or three minutes, the rest of you will talk to each other—not to the subject—about his good qualities, as best you can.
—After you're finished talking about him, go to the next team member, and so on, until everyone has heard him- or herself described.

There are a few more things that should be kept in mind.

In your group there will be at least one rescuer. A rescuer fears something will happen to make the subject feel bad. She will hear the initial silence and start to praise at a rapid pace. I happen to be one of these people myself. Rescuers won't let anybody else talk, just in case they might not talk. The rule here is that a rescuer is not allowed to speak until last. Even if there should be thirty seconds of dead silence, enough to make a rescuer start weeping, it is essential to take time to think, to make sure that the quiet people get a chance to contribute. They have important things to say. Then when everyone is done, the rescuer can rush in and patch up all the holes if she wants to.

Only one person has to wait longer than the rescuer to speak. That's anyone in the group who happens to know the person on the hot seat. Their unfair advantage is actually a disadvantage, for they feel obliged to say expected things. After listening to strangers assess a close friend, they usually come up with fresh insights, surprising both themselves and their friend.

The other key rules for the praisers are:

—Describe assets only. No constructive criticism.
—Be specific. You'll feel like a phony when you praise a stranger unless you target your praise with careful accuracy.

Be warned—once you've said all the specific things you can, like "George seems well organized" or "creative" or "a wonderful listener" or "has a great laugh," you may start to run dry. This is the time to turn your intuition loose and get playful. You might say, "Why do I see Evelyn playing a grand piano in a bikini?" "Somehow I can imagine Ed running away and joining the circus." Use your instincts. Frequently you'll hit on just the detail that makes the difference, and amaze the subject with your insights.

The rules for the subject in the hot seat:

—Write everything down, as dutifully as a secretary taking dictation. Write legibly. You will be surprised how valuable that piece of paper will be to you. (I saved mine for years, and still regret losing it.)
—Don't respond to what you hear. Remember, you're overhearing people discuss you. Just sit there and take it.
—Use sign language communication if you can't hear clearly what's being said (cup your hand to your ear for "louder," wave your hand for "slower").

When everyone is finished, you simply turn around—no comment—and the next person turns his or her back. After being the one in the hot seat, your head will be spinning a little, and you won't quite be able to get into the next conversation right away, but you will have a few moments of anonymity as the attention moves away, and you'll need them. Join in after a minute or so.

That's it. Try it out. You'll never forget it. Some common reactions to Assets Feedback:

—"Where have you all been all my life!"
—"Embarrassing!"
—"I loved having a chance to tell other people what's good about them." (How often do we get to do that?)
—"How could they see the person I was hiding?"
—"I just think of myself as a cook and mother, and nobody saw me as that."

This is everybody's favorite exercise. "It just keeps on amazing me," says career developer Jeannie Schatzki, who organizes teams and acts as coach for the first six meetings. "It's such an artificial exercise when most of the people don't know each other. But everyone loves it. Time after time it breaks the ice and makes people feel good. In the evaluations I have them do at the sixth meeting, they remember that the first thing that happened in the team was having people tell them good things about themselves. It's amazing how much we all seem to need that." This exercise makes you feel valuable and unique. If you choose a goal now, it will be a goal worthy of you.

Now you can pick what you really want.

And now, your team really wants you to get it.

Now you are a Success Team.

Your first team meeting is essentially over after the assets exercise. There are just two or three more things to do:

1. Give your team a name, if you want to. (Strictly optional—some people think it's corny, others think it's fun and creates team spirit. I've known teams that called themselves the Energizers, the Powerhouse Five, the Get Set.)
2. Assign homework. This is going to be a regular feature of teamwork. Your assignment for the second meeting is:

   —Think of something you really want—to do, to be, to have—and haven't been able to get by yourself.
   —If you're not sure what you want, think about the goalsearch questions in this book (p. 39), and/or:
   —Draw up a list of the things you'd be doing in Paradise (p. 36), and/or:
   —Read the Stylesearch and Goalsearch chapters in *Wishcraft* (Chapters 3 and 4). Stylesearch includes seven imagination exercises designed to help you search your personal style for clues to what you'd love to do. Goalsearch helps you shape those clues into a tangible goal. Some teams like to work on the imagination exercises at home; bring them in and discuss their discoveries.

3. Set a date, time and place for your second (goalsetting) meeting. (Even if your team will be meeting every other week, try to make the goalsetting meeting a week after the team-building meeting. You are now creating momentum for the months to come.) Compare schedules, and try to set a regular meeting time that will work for all of you. Keep in mind that perfect attendance may not be possible, but poor attendance will end your team.

That's the first meeting of your Success Team. The second meeting will be dedicated to goalsetting.

11...

How to Run a Success Team, the Second Meeting: Goalsetting

First, I want to give you the rules I mentioned to you. They look very simple, but they're at the heart of your team's success.

START TEAM MEETINGS ON TIME

There's a problem with Success Teams: they're so enjoyable that you can forget they mean business. At a team meeting you may feel as if you're at a party, but don't be fooled: this is a business meeting for your personal goals. You know that when you have a business meeting at work, or a meeting with your child's teacher, you're prepared and you're on time. Success Teams take your own business—your heart's desire—just that seriously. The only way to combine the festivity that makes teams fun with the seriousness that makes them work is to keep meetings very structured in regard to time. So:

—Begin promptly at the specified time, whether or not everyone has arrived.
—If someone is late, he has to join the meeting in progress. Don't take time out to backtrack or update.
—Members should understand that it's part of their commitment to their teammates to be on time. Whenever

117

someone is late, someone has to brainstorm without the
benefit of the full team.

Some teams have come up with an improvement: they ask
people to come at, say, 2:30, and then start the business meeting
at 3:00. That gives everyone a chance to say hello, and makes
it likelier that they'll all be there by the time the team gets to
work.

The second important rule is:

SET TIME LIMITS FOR EACH PERSON

If there are five of you, twenty minutes each is the absolute
limit. If there are six, fifteen minutes. Bring a clock timer. This
is more important than it may appear.

There are a number of problems that can sabotage a team
over time:

—One member may need so much attention that others
   get neglected.
—People may become such good friends that they have
   trouble getting down to business.
—We often have the impulse to solve the first person's
   problems perfectly before moving on to the second. Then
   there's not enough time.

Every one of these problems can be stopped with a clock
timer. You might misuse your allotted time once or twice, but
you won't let it happen a third time. The clock timer is the real
top sergeant in a leaderless group, and will do more to guarantee your team's effectiveness than any other kind of control.

Now to the work of the second team meeting: setting your
goal. Your homework for the week was to do some thinking
about what you want.

Sometimes you come into a Success Team with a very clear
idea of what that goal is. In that case, this meeting will help
you to clarify the obstacles—to narrow them down and to name

them. This takes your goal from appearing impossible to being merely problematic.

Often, though, you come into a Success Team not knowing what your goal is. This session will help you begin to create, or remember, your personal dream.

There are no rules about what a goal should be. Yours may be vocational, avocational, or strictly personal. Some team members are concerned with improving their jobs or careers. But sometimes you'll find that a person's dream is completely different from her job. Someone who wants to be a poet may be earning her living as a secretary. This does not necessarily signal a career change. There are many people who are working at pleasant, undemanding jobs, which makes it possible for them to do what they love after hours. Think carefully before you decide to make a living from your dream. Writing, painting, gardening for money means you can't do what you want, you must meet someone else's requirements. Remember, Albert Einstein liked being a patent clerk.

There are others who want to make money doing what they love, but aren't ready yet. They need to gain experience doing it on the side before they risk committing their lives. Unless you happen to have a trust fund or a rich spouse, I don't advise you to quit your job to start a graphics business until you've been doing it part-time successfully for a while.

Now your goalsetting meeting begins.
Pick someone to go first, and set the timer.
The team asks the goalsetter:

—What do you want?

After she or he answers, they ask:

—What's the problem?

If the goalsetter knows what he wants, his teammates work with him in three ways:

1. They help him set a target: a tangible version of his goal that can be achieved by a specific date, his target date.

For instance, if the answer to "What do you want?" is "To be an actor," that is not yet concrete enough to be achieved by a certain date. An aspiring actor's target might be "to complete an acting class in the next two months" or "to get an agent by summer" or "to get a part in a showcase." If the person's goal is "to open my own tennis shop," the target could be "to open my own tennis shop eighteen months from now."

The goalsetter should choose a target date that seems possible but not too distant. Target dates can always be renegotiated, but we all need the pressure of a deadline to make our goals real.

2. The team goes to work on the goalsetter's problem or problems, helping him transform big, vague obstacles, such as "money," into precise ones—such as "a $15,000 down payment" or "a student loan for design school" —that can be tackled strategically.

3. They help the goalsetter plan backward to first steps that he can take in the coming week. "What do I have to do to get a student loan? Apply for one. What do I have to do before I can do that? Go to the financial-aid office for information and application forms. Can I do that this week? Yes."

A would-be actor's first steps could be: "Call friends to find a photographer for a head shot"; "Call acting schools to ask about classes"; "Set up an interview with a working actor to ask about agents"; etc. A would-be entrepreneur's could be: "Open savings account for starting capital"; "Order wholesale tennis supply catalogues"; "Set up an interview with a retail shop owner"; "Call Small Business Administration for loan info"; etc.

It is the team's job to help the goalsetter come up with really useful first steps.

It is the goalsetter's job to:

—Write all these steps down on a piece of paper.
—Schedule as many steps as he realistically can do in the coming week into specific dates in his pocket calendar. These are business appointments, which the team expects to hear about at the next meeting.

If any of the first steps seem difficult or frightening, the goalsetter can pick a crisis-call buddy from among his teammates, and schedule a morale-boosting phone call. Calls can go either way: the helping teammate can call and say, "Got your shoes on? Get out there and jog," or the person on the firing line can call the supporter and say, "Well, here goes nothing—I'm starting to write." Teammates can also rehearse each other for phone calls and interviews. If there's not enough time during the brainstorming period, use open time at the end of the meeting or make a date with teammates for the purpose of rehearsing.

That completes the first person's turn. When the timer rings, move on to the next.

If the goalsetter doesn't know what she wants, she can make it her goal to find a goal. This is a project in itself, and an important one. Here's how the team can help:

—Have the goalsetter read her Paradise list out loud. Try to invent goals that combine two or more items on the list. See if she finds them interesting.
—Ask the goalsetter any of the goalsearch questions I've suggested—and any others you can think of:
  —"If we could wave a magic wand and give you something that would make you really happy, what would it be?"
  —"What do you do naturally—almost effortlessly?"
  —"What did you love to do as a child?" (Some people who are happiest with their work are still doing what they loved to do as children. Sue Hadley says her former husband "remembered stringing a string between two trees and putting a blanket over it, and the sense of power he had, creating that shelter and getting out of the rain." He's now an architect! Sue, who grew up to be a career educator, recalls how she "used to watch people in the malls while my mother was shopping, and wonder what made them happy and what made them sad.")
  —"What was your childhood dream?" Adults who aren't sure what they want can often remember an unfulfilled childhood dream or ambition. "I wanted to be

an artist . . . a doctor . . . an astronaut . . . a jockey."
Maybe they still do! Or the childhood dream may no
longer be within reach—at forty-four or sixty-four, it's
too late to become a ballerina, big-league baseball player,
or concert violinist—but it's still a clue to something
you love and probably have talent for. The team's job
is to help you identify the essence of that dream (what
in *Wishcraft* I called the touchstone)—and then create
a goal that delivers that essence in attainable form.

Here's how the team can spot a secret wish:

—Listen for things like, "This is really stupid, but . . ."
That's when the real goal is coming. That's what people
say when they're about to tell the truth.
—Watch for the goalsetter's eyes to light up. I let people
keep talking till I see The Look. I've described The Look
on p. 38. It's the same shining, soft look people get in
their eyes when they talk about someone they love.
—Watch the goalsetter's body language. Team coach Jeannie Schatzki says, "You can train the team to notice when
people are talking about what they really want to do—
how they light up and lean forward, how their whole
demeanor changes and their voice gets animated. And
conversely, if they start talking about what they think
they should do, or what is the practical thing to do, their
shoulders slump and their voice sounds heavy and resigned."

If team brainstorming comes up with a goal that the goalsetter
would like to try, she should leave the goalsetting meeting with
some first steps. If the goalsearch process is going to take more
time, the goalsetter's homework might be to write down childhood memories; to do some of the imagination exercises in the
Stylesearch chapter of *Wishcraft*; or to research possible goals.
(For example, someone who loved animals might have first
steps like, "Go to library and read about women in veterinary
medicine;" "Interview zookeepers;" "Interview a veterinarian's
assistant;" "Call animal shelters, wildlife organizations, or local
forest preserves and ask if they need help.")

If the goalsetter has more than one goal, have him pick just one to practice the *Teamworks!* techniques on. Once his planning and action skills are honed, he'll be able to handle multiple goals. But at the beginning, two goals tend to use up too much team time and divide efforts. Whenever he has something important and frightening to do on one goal, he'll switch to the other.

People who want to work on many goals at the same time usually suffer from what I call time hysteria. "I want to be a singer and go to Spain and learn French and I want to do it all right away!" "Why?" I ask. "Is the world ending tomorrow?" "No, but I've wasted so much time already!" They try to slice their time into too many pieces and wind up making themselves frantic. (That was always my failing. I understand it all too well.)

This kind of panic is most common in people who've always been interrupted by necessity. They have never had the experience of moving steadily over time toward one goal. Once you've had that experience—with your team's help—you know you can do it again, and the breathless impatience subsides. Time becomes a friend. So tell any member of your team who has more than one goal: start with one. No need to write off the others. Plant the seeds now for a goal you won't get to for five years. You've probably got another one that you can do for a week out of every year, and others you can do on an occasional weekend. And then there are the ones you work on all the time, quietly—like singing in the shower or reading about Greece. They just fit themselves in when the impatience goes away.

At the end of the goalsetting meeting, set your team target date—the latest target date of any team member, or the amount of time you're all willing to commit to—six months, eight months, a year. When that date arrives, you'll see what you've accomplished. Then you can decide whether to disband or set new goals. Do your best to keep meeting until your team target date.

By the end of the goalsetting meeting, each member of your Success Team should have first steps scheduled into his or her pocket calendar for the coming week. You should also have each other's planned actions written down. Any crisis calls or rehearsals you've promised each other should be entered in your pocket calendars, too.

Now, you're going to find out what a Success Team is best at: action!

12...

How to Run a Success Team: The Third and All Subsequent Meetings

HOW OFTEN SHOULD YOUR SUCCESS TEAM MEET?

Many successful teams meet weekly. Some meet every other week, but that seems to be the outer limit. If more than two weeks go by between meetings, continuity is lost, and the team unravels. (There's an exception to every rule. One successful team in the Boston area meets once a month—and is still going strong after two years. But this team started out meeting weekly, and didn't cut back till the bonds of mutual commitment were strong.)

So: weekly or biweekly?

Your choice will depend on how intensive a support system you feel you need—and how busy you all are. Some teams start out meeting weekly, when the process is new. After some months, they get a little burned out on the weekly schedule, and they cut back to twice a month.

HOW LONG IS A TYPICAL TEAM MEETING?

I recommend that people keep the business part of the meeting to one and a half hours. In my experience, when each person gets more than twenty minutes, people start to ramble, and the crisp, businesslike focus of the meeting can get lost.

However . . . some people who wrote to me about their experiences in Success Teams said that their team members liked to have more time: at least twenty minutes, or better yet, half an hour! And their typical team meetings were lasting at least two hours.

So I suggest you experiment with the individual time limits. Start out with fifteen minutes each, and if that doesn't feel like enough after a couple of meetings, try adding five minutes to the central (Teamwork) piece of your time (you'll learn what that is in a minute). You'll really appreciate those extra five minutes, and you'll make much better use of them than you would if you'd had them all along.

FORMAT FOR THE REGULAR TEAM MEETING:

Each person gets fifteen (or twenty) minutes, divided up as follows:

FIVE MINUTES: HOMEWORK REPORT

Tell what you did—and didn't do—since the last meeting. What worked? What didn't? What progress did you make toward your goal? Where were you blocked, and why?

This simple act of reporting in is one of the ways that your team will help you reach your goals. It creates accountability. Someone else cares whether you did it or not—the way your boss at work cares whether you wrote that report—except that your boss at work expects you to meet his goals, the company's goals, while this boss, your team, insists that you meet your goals! It works like magic. People who've been stuck on a project for years find that having Success Team accountability is the first thing that's ever enabled them to get going—and keep going.

"Work-wise, I really like what I do, and I didn't have any

problem progressing there," said Framingham, Mass. human-resources consultant Kathleen Greer. "But I was also trying to work on a book, and it was always getting put on the back burner. So I used the team to structure me. I would do things such as make a commitment to the team to have a chapter done, or some piece of it, and then bring it in. It really helped— because I didn't like showing up at the meeting and having to tell them I didn't do it! They also gave me valuable feedback." Unfortunately, after eighteen months, Kathy's team broke up because of other time commitments—"and when the team stopped, so did the book!"

The second segment of each team member's time is:

FIVE (OR TEN) MINUTES: TEAMWORK

How can the team help you?

Important: "Let the person talking ask for what *they* want," said Boston advertising director Arlene S. "When our team first started, someone would talk about a problem they'd had, and everyone else would immediately jump in with what that person should do. You have to let the person talk, and you listen. Don't assume that you know what she or he is going to ask for." During your teamwork time, the total focus of the team is on you, your goal, and the problems you've run into. Here are some of the kinds of help you can ask for:

BRAINSTORMING

The team can come up with bright ideas for what to do next, take what didn't work and strategize how to make it work, or dream up alternatives. "No putting down. No trashing," cautions team veteran Virginia C. "Never negatively criticizing someone's attempt is enormously important, because when someone gets put down, it's very hard for them to go on. What our team would suggest instead, if someone didn't do their assignment, or it didn't work, was that it was the wrong assignment. It wasn't that the person was wrong. We had to find an assignment that they were more comfortable with."

That's an instinctive attitude which is pure genius! Adapting your tasks to suit who you really are at any given time looks like coddling to the Spartans or Puritans among us, but in fact, it is the most efficient method of getting the best out of people. Respecting who you are, not who you ought to be, and adapting plans to that reality, requires a viewpoint that is more deeply philosophical and ethical than you might imagine.

For one thing, it teaches both the modesty and realism that come from understanding your limits. We would be gods, we're taught that we should aspire to perfection—while always denigrating our efforts with true humility! But we are not gods, we are humans, and not enough attention has been paid to how we actually function best, rather than to how we should function best. "Should" can be a dangerous word. A whole world has been built on it. All the sixties and seventies trends toward Eastern religion are a reflection of how we're beginning to sense that "should" is not always right and "is" has some real value.

I'm not a Zen Buddhist, I'm a hopelessly Western go-getter with a trace of Ferdinand the Bull in me (remember him? He didn't want to fight. He just wanted to smell the flowers). I know that to attain any goal—being rich and successful, or spreading the word, or learning Greek like I.F. Stone—I'll get where I want to go more by understanding my real nature, my real limits, than by prodding myself to Herculean tasks and punishing myself when I don't achieve them. To move forward is important. To move forward swiftly in the hardest way imaginable is not.

So coddling can be surprisingly efficient, and goading is usually not!

Suppose, however, that a person is capable of more than you're demanding, and their lack of movement is no more than a kind of protest? What if they're their own worst enemy? Suppose they need to be pushed, to be told "You can do it!" —and you're unwittingly letting them down by coddling them?

Well, surprise. They'll get impatient with being coddled, and demand more of themselves after a while. It's a self-correcting error. Especially if they're in a team and see others progressing each week.

So Virginia's team got it right, and that has to be one of the reasons why it has such a wonderful record of achievement. Now back to the ways your team can help you:

RESOURCING AND BARN-RAISING

Contacts, connections, concrete suggestions: what to read, who to call, who can teach you about it, where to find it. Give specific information: the title of that sensational book on giving presentations, the name and phone number of your aunt who speaks Portuguese. Virginia C. offered a variation: "From time to time we'd have a meeting where we would all bring in our address books, and we would go through them to see if we knew anybody who would be good for another teammate—a contact of some sort."

SKILL SHARING

The variety in your team really pays off when team members offer each other the benefit of their professional or amateur skills. Some of the best success stories are born of a lucky fit between what one teammate needs and what another one knows. For instance:

Diane C., a writer and the editor of a Boston-area alumni magazine, had made it her goal to ask for a raise. Her teammate Kathleen Greer is a human-resources consultant to corporations. "As an outgrowth of the group, Kathy and I met together and did a practice session," says Diane. "She used her professional skills to coach me, and we even videotaped it. I watched it and learned to smile more!" Diane got her raise. Now she's going for her next one.

"I could draw like a million bucks, but I didn't know how to keep books at all," said Virginia C., who was setting up her own freelance business as a medical illustrator. "The graphic artist on my team had been on her own for years and was very businesslike. She came over and spent an entire day with me. She showed me how to project what my needs would be for the next year, so I could figure out what I had to earn, and then how to keep records, so that when you go to the tax accountant, it's logical and clear."

Annemarie P. brought a knotty problem to her team: she'd been wanting to move out of New York City with her young son for a long time, but she didn't know where she wanted to go. With the team's help, "I got much more focused than I'd ever been before," says Annemarie. "I made a whole list of criteria about where I wanted to be. It had to have a town center, so the suburbs were out; it had to have a diverse group of people; it had to be a certain size, under 25,000; I wanted to live around farms, but New England was too cold for me; and it had to have a lot of outdoor activity." One of Annemarie's teammates, Phyllis W., was a holistic healer. Using the skills of her profession, Phyllis questioned and counseled Annemarie to help her figure out where her unconscious preferences were pointing her. It looked more and more like Taos, New Mexico.

"I went out there to visit, and right away I met a million welcoming people," says Annemarie. "I had visited lots of other places, and that had never happened to me before. I also found somebody I could stay with when I moved out." Within a month, Annemarie, who'd been stuck for so long, had made the move. It transformed her life. "Things I thought were too extraordinary for me to want are so *simple* here," she says. "I'm working on my garden. I'm going to have chickens. We live right next to horses, so we can ride. And for my son it's just great. He's super-independent here." Annemarie feels she was meant to live in Taos, but she's not sure that, without Phyllis's help, she would have discovered that. Phyllis, in turn, got assistance with advertising and brochures from another team-mate, skilled in public relations.

Hayward, California, jewelry designer Christofer A. told of a teammate who was "a registered nurse with her own health and nutritional counseling business. Janice came to the group looking for ways to expand her client base. In our sessions she worked on ways to advertise, ways to approach health prac-titioners who could refer clients to her, ways to approach com-munity groups as a speaker. She put a brochure together with the help of another member of the group who did the graphics!"

A career counselor who is coaching teams can make his or her professional skills available to team members as part of what they're paying for. Everyone else, take to heart this wise caveat from Eugene, Oregon, networker Meta H.: "It is im-portant to offer only those resources which you feel like offer-ing. It is not appropriate to offer skills which you no longer enjoy using (like a typist who is tired of typing), nor to offer for free skills for which you wish to be paid. . . . It is important to say no promptly, firmly, and without guilt when someone asks for help which you prefer not to give, or offers help which you prefer not to receive. . . . Honest responses greatly increase our freedom to ask and to offer whatever occurs to us." In other words, knowing how to say no will make you a more generous person!

REHEARSAL

"I was having a price problem with one of my clients," says Virginia C. "It was a serious problem. I had worked with this doctor for years, and we'd been friends, but it had come time for me to raise my prices, and when my bill came, he really was not prepared to deal with it. And I was scared. I didn't feel that I could stand up to him. I just wanted to crawl in a hole and pull the cover over my head. So I brought it to the group, and they role-played with me. We went through every possible conversation that I could have with this doctor, and by the time we finished, I was much more relaxed; I was actually looking forward to facing it!" The group also suggested that Virginia find someone to mediate. So she brought along a fellow medical illustrator, and the dispute was resolved—in her favor. "It could have been a disaster," she says. Instead, she still works with that doctor—and is still friends with him.

HARD TIMES

Sometimes a team member needs to use most of the teamwork time for a gripe session (p. 93). When a team member talks in a heavy, hopeless voice about how hard things have been this week, but he waves away every suggestion, you know he's a candidate for a Hard Times session.

Never try to talk anyone out of a bad mood. You'll only wear yourself out and make the other person more resistant. Instead, encourage negativity. Invite the person to indulge in a really creative complaining session. Then cheer the complainer on! Applaud creative negativity. This gives him a chance to ventilate the tension that can build up when anyone undertakes a high-risk enterprise. Your teammate may simply need time out from the stress of forward motion. Discouragement can mask rebellion, and Hard Times gives the rebel a chance to come out. Watch the person's mood shoot up when he's allowed to change "I can't" into "I won't!" (He can later back down from this position and get back to work.)

INTENSIVE CARE

If a teammate is approaching a crisis—she has something important to do and is blocked, or too scared to do it—the team can:

- —set up a crisis call schedule: arrange for someone to call the person just before and just after she sits down to write or to make that phone call (see Procrastinators Anonymous, p. 200, for the most intensive form of intensive care)
- —take turns sitting in the next room while the person practices the cello or writes
- —arrange to accompany him or her to the door of the interview/doctor's office/classroom/health club

The appropriate tone here is sympathetic toughness. The point is to get the person over the hurdle: she is not allowed to back out. "There were a couple of acting classes I really wanted to take," Marcia J. said. "I signed up for them, and I told the group, 'Okay, I'm really going.' And I couldn't go to the first meeting—I was so intimidated! I came back to the team and said, 'You know, my father wasn't feeling well, and my cat was ill . . .' I had been practicing that story all day. The team didn't but it. They said, 'It sounds like you're really stalling.' They said, 'We'll call you before,' and they made sure that I had people to call. I went to the course, and I had a great time." "We got to know each other's tricks and defenses and excuses," said Derek C., "and we would call each other on that on a fairly regular basis."

The team's job is to take away excuses and in their place, give support.

And now, the third and final segment of each person's time:

FIVE MINUTES: HOMEWORK ASSIGNMENT

(LaVaun Maier of Milwaukie, Oregon, calls this the action commitment for the next meeting.) Decide what you plan to do in the next week (or two). Write steps—and any crisis calls or meetings with teammates—into specific dates in your pocket calendar. (Artist Karen R.'s Los Angeles teammates agreed that they would call each other at least once a week. Sometimes a team member would say, "This week I need to talk to someone every day.")

Important: Your teammates also write down what you are planning to do. They are going to ask you about it at the next meeting. They will not conveniently forget. It's important to know that a friendly person is keeping track of you. In some way they're present in your life all week long, watching out for you. Their anticipation of and enthusiasm for your weekly progress are harder to resist than the toughest taskmaster.

Remember the clock timer. You will soon get very efficient at doing what you need to do within your fifteen (or twenty) minutes. When the timer rings, go on to the next person. Leave any unfinished business for the end of the meeting.

Some variations on the basic team-meeting format:

"At the beginning of the meeting, we'll ask if anyone has a major crisis, and if so, they immediately talk about that, before everyone gets their half hour." (Derek C.)

"We started every meeting by going around the group, asking people to 'Tell us any considerations that are keeping you from being present here. Is there anything on anybody's mind that might interfere or distract?' People would say things like, 'I feel lousy because I talked nasty to my kid' or 'I'm worried about my condominium closing' or 'I don't want to be here tonight. I want to watch *L.A. Law.*' After saying those things out loud, we'd be much more present." (Karen R. and Stella M.)

"If we have a problem we'll call each other, and if necessary we'll call an emergency session." (Derek C.)

LaVaun Maier starts her biweekly team meetings by having members fill out a Reflection Question Sheet, which they then share in twos before speaking to the whole group:

My goal this quarter:
What I planned to do in the past two weeks:
What I did in the past two weeks:
How I feel about what I did or didn't do:
What I learned:
What I need from the group tonight (brainstorming, barn-raising, hard times, chance to clarify, help in writing an affirmation, etc.):
At the end of meeting: action commitment for coming two weeks

Christofer A., who facilitated all her team's meetings in her home, would "put all the pertinent information on the computer during the meeting. At the end of the meeting, each member got a printout, making it much easier to follow up on one another the next time."

A similar accountability strategy: a Minneapolis-St. Paul team assigned one member each week to keep minutes. At the beginning of the next meeting, copies of the minutes were handed out. Their format:

Place of Meeting: (name & address)
Time of Meeting: (date & time)
Members Present: (names)
Members Absent: (names)

I. Susan S. reported as follows:
1. Quit job.
2. Rewrite résumé for next week.
3. Call temporary agency.
(etc.)

II. Jeri W. reported as follows:
1. Organ lesson this Thursday.
2. Call organ repair service.
3. Found two books on inventions. Have read one.
4. Have to record idea for invention:
    a. see lawyer

      b. patent search
      c. sketch or drawing
   (etc.)
III. Marge F. reported by telephone:
   1. Unable to make it due to a conflict with another meeting
   2. Will make a tape recording of poetry reading and send it with Jeri to the talent show on Wednesday night
   (etc.)

This brings us to the unavoidable issue of absenteeism—as well as other common problems Success Teams (like other kinds of groups) run into:

—leadership conflicts
—emotional upsets brought to team meetings (setting the strategy/support group function aside)
—loss and addition of members
—the occasional loss of momentum

There are rules for coping with all these problems; they can only sink your team if you're unprepared for them. The troubleshooting tips in the next chapter have been garnered from experience—not only my own, but that of people all over the country who've told me about their teams' successes and stumbling blocks.

13...

How to Run a Success Team: Team Troubleshooting

There are seven common problems that afflict voluntary, leaderless groups, and Success Teams are no exception. Here are the best ways to deal with them.

1. Mixing pleasure with business. The voices of people whose teams succumbed to this temptation are a rueful little hymn to the rules. "I previously had a very small group using your book, and it had fallen apart," wrote D. DABy F. of Beverly Hills, California. "I had violated your principles about sticking to a firm structure, and in addition had mixed social interplay with the meetings." "We were still meeting every week, but nobody was going anywhere," Marcia J. recalled of her New York City team's demise after five months. "We'd just gripe and decide who we wanted to marry when we grew up. And I thought, 'What a waste of time. I'm just sitting here entertaining people in my living room.' "

"First of all there were eight people, so the number was unwieldy," Jane Shuman of Springfield, Illinois, said of her first team. "Second of all, we met over lunch, so we were in the 'social mode,' and we kept trying to meet in environments where there were phone interruptions. Since it was a lunchtime thing, people would come late and leave early, and that broke up the group process. Finally that group dwindled down from eight to four, and the four of us began to meet for two hours every other Sunday evening, which gave us the time we needed, and the peace. We each took a half hour, so we really put the structure in there that we needed, and that worked better."

A Success Team is not a bunch of buddies sitting around having coffee. We're using hardheaded business methods to achieve personal dreams—and they only work if you're businesslike about them.

2. Irregular or infrequent meetings. "We met weekly, usually Sundays, for two to three hours, and we continued this pattern for about two months," wrote Ronda H. of Skokie, Illinois. "From that point on, we found it too difficult to schedule regularly, so we met sporadically and our meetings became less focused."

"Meeting once a month was, I think, not enough," said Boston computer professional Laurie Z. "It was too long between meetings to hold accountability. We assigned each other tasks to do, and if you didn't do them by the next meeting, you just kind of lost sight of the meaning of it all." Laurie's team also met irregularly, as another member, alumni magazine editor Diane C., recalled: "We kept changing the time, because somebody couldn't come, or maybe it would snow, so we'd postpone a meeting . . . Then it got less frequent"—and finally petered out.

Having learned from her first group's lack of structure, D. DABy F. wrote, "This time I established a firm time and a firm day—in our case it's 6:30 P.M. on Tuesday nights." That group has now been meeting for several months.

It's a matter of priorities. Setting a firm time and a firm day, weekly or every other week, makes your team meeting a solid commitment that you'll make time for. As busy as you are, remember that the commitment to your teammates is also a commitment to yourself. If you're pursuing personal goals, that commitment needs to be acted on regularly. It's the only thing that gives our own interests a fighting chance among all the competing needs and demands of our lives.

3. Absenteeism. That said, we have to face facts: there will be times when one or more of you simply can't make it to a meeting. In one set of minutes I've seen, reasons why team members had to be absent included a slipped disk, conflict with another meeting, a child's event at school, a vacation, problems with the car, and a family tragedy. We lead crowded lives, and it's quite an accomplishment to even try to fit one more commitment in. To honor it flawlessly is almost impossible.

A team can (and must) take occasional absences, but not a plague of them. If fewer than three or four members show up for a majority of your meetings, your team is fading. I suggested you start out with six to eight people so that, allowing for attrition, you end up with a core of four or five who are strongly committed to the team. When a particular member is absent more than she or he is present, that person obviously isn't able or willing to give the team priority, and is usually on the way out.

Sometimes people just bite off more than they can chew; sometimes their circumstances change unexpectedly; and sometimes they discover that they're not cut out for the team process, or that they need a faster or slower team. Ideally, natural selection will whittle your initial group down to a good, compact, lasting team—or, if it gets whittled down too far, you can invite one or two likely people to join.

Within your core team, a good way to handle necessary absences is to have the missing member phone in during the meeting. An enthusiastic team member usually is more than willing to do this. (If you have a speakerphone so everyone can hear and talk at the same time, so much the better.) That way, continuity is maintained. Reporting in helps the absent member stay on track, reminds that person of the team's warm support, and reaffirms the commitment to be there for each other. Though a missing member can't help out with brainstorming over the phone, she can ask teammates how their week's homework went, as well as tell briefly about her own triumphs and traumas.

An alternative method of maintaining continuity is suggested by D. DABy F.: "The facilitator for that week [see Rotating Leadership, p. 141] is responsible for contacting the members who were not at the meeting."

If one or more members are frequently absent, it's a good

idea to sit down with the absentee(s)—or call them on the phone if they've really disappeared—and ask what's going on.

—Why have they been having so much trouble getting to meetings? (The reasons may be practical or emotional— or emotional disguised as practical. The point is not to pressure or interrogate your teammate, but simply to give him or her a fresh chance to make use of the team's support.)
—Do they still want to be a part of the team?
—If so, how can we help them make more meetings?
—If not, the team now knows clearly who's in it and who's not. You won't keep waiting for someone who's not coming.

4. Losing members and adding new ones. Three people is really the bare minimum for a team, and four is a better number for absorbing occasional absenteeism. (Two people who really prefer working one-on-one to a group can set up a buddy system—see p. 182—but the rules are a little different.) If you've lost members and are down to a number that you feel endangers your survival as a team, you can recruit replacements from among your friends and acquaintances. By now you'll know even better what kind of people to look for. "There was someone who dropped out very early on, and we decided it was nice to have five people, so I invited another friend of mine, and she came in, as I thought she would," said Massachusetts actor/director Derek C.

Bringing someone new into your team in midstream requires the team's input—a tip I can give you thanks to the sad experience of D. DABy F. "When I brought in the first new member to replace one member who had dropped out," wrote DABy, "the group was vocally negative for not being asked in advance, and the new person was uninformed about our group. This made my guest uncomfortable, and she never returned. However, at the next meeting, we set up a new rule (everything serves a function). The new-member rule is that you inform the group the week before that you want to bring someone in, so they expect it. The new person is expected to have read

Wishcraft up to the point where the group has reached. [DABy's group was working through *Wishcraft* chapter by chapter; you could assign parts of it or *Teamworks!* to help a new team member catch up.] This familiarizes the new person with the uniqueness of the group and our own terminology."

5. The leadership question. This is the one of the most important issues affecting team success and survival. The leadership dilemma can be stated in a nutshell:

—Some teams feel most cohesive and motivated when they have a leader—whether it's a natural leader who's emerged from the team itself, or a career counselor coaching an introductory series of meetings. But then other problems can arise:

—The team becomes dependent on the career counselor/ leader, and when she or he leaves, the team tends to drift; *or*:

—If a natural leader has taken charge of the team—or a rescuer, one of those people who feel obliged to take responsibility for any problems—he may come to feel burdened. If he withdraws from the leadership role, the team may fall apart; *or*:

—Other team members may resent the takeover, since it happened without their consent.

Marlissa M., who got her dream job at a public-TV station with her team's support, remembers the authority vacuum in the team when its professional coach had finished her six sessions. "We'd become close, and no one felt like assuming the responsibility of instigating a direction," says Marlissa. "We were trying to be supportive to each other. No one felt like enforcing anything on anyone else. And the enforcing was important: we really needed to do our homework every week. The leader had held people to that. We were directionless after she left. We all felt afterward that we needed stronger guidelines for keeping going."

Similar problems can afflict a team that has learned to lean on a natural leader, one appointed from within the team by the workings of group dynamics. A team that formed after a sem-

inar I did in Boston lasted a year and a half—till its unacknow-
ledged leader burned out. Everyone agreed who she was:
Framingham, Mass. personnel consultant Kathleen Greer, a
superb organizer and resource person.

"The key to our team's success was Kathy," said Diane C.
"She would do the calling and set up the times. She had so
much to offer people in practical ways, and she is very generous
in giving her time and her talents. The reason the team broke
up is that Kathy said she no longer could be the—well, she
always insists she was not the leader, and would not be the
leader, but in fact she was." Banker David E. agreed: "The team
needs someone to schedule meetings, to find a place to meet,
to remind people, and so forth. Kathleen did all that for a while,
and she kept saying, 'I'm not going to keep doing this forever.
Someone else has got to take over.' " "This time when she said
it, she meant it," said Diane C. "She's had a change in her
schedule, and she's much busier. So I said I was going to pick
it up and do it, but I haven't. And no one else did." Kathy's
teammates are now regretful about their willingness to let her
do the organizational work—and to let their team fade away
when she could no longer do it.

There are several ways to solve this problem. Try them, until
you find the balance of leadership and democracy that works
best for your team.

—Teams that really prefer having a leader can simply hire
 one for the life of the team. Members pay a weekly fee
 for a career counselor's services.
—Some teams set up a floating chairmanship. They hold
 meetings at each member's home for a month, and during that month the host is responsible for any administrative issues, phone calls, and timekeeping. This is
 good training for people unaccustomed to having authority. It's also a way to teach rescuers to let go. Because
 the leader is also the host, the most eager rescuer will
 usually remember not to take over.
—Other teams choose to rotate leadership even more often.
 "We met every week, and there'd be cheese and crackers
 on the table, maybe a little wine, and the person in
 whose house we met was the person who sort of led

that week," says Virginia C. "We were all peers, so that no one was ever the boss. I liked that very much."

—Occasionally, the role of timekeeper and rulekeeper will naturally fall to one team member, who just cares the most or does it best. "You need someone to keep the group on purpose—if one member goes off on a long story, to bring them back and say, 'Answer the question,' " says Los Angeles writer Stella M. "In our team, it's me a lot, because I'm good at that." Advertising director Arlene S. plays a similar role in her team: "I'm the clock-watcher, rule-setter, custodian of the group. I'm good at it, and it's important to me to keep on a time schedule, because we meet at 7 P.M., go home at 10, and I'm up at 5 A.M. So I want people to get to the point. I get some resistance, but mostly it's accepted." (It's okay for one person to play this role, as long as it works. If either the clock-watcher or the other team members start to resent the situation, it's time to rotate the role.)

The most crucial item in a leaderless team is the clock timer. It's a magic charm against anarchy. I have a little formula for this:

—The rules *are* the leader.

As long as everyone agrees to stick to the rules of team structure—using the timer, starting meetings on time, doing homework—you won't lose momentum. And once this agreement is in place, no one has to enforce. Structure replaces authority, maintaining equality among members of the team.

You'll find that structure is surprisingly welcome. "I've never had anybody say the meeting was too structured or rigid," says team coach Jeannie Schatzki. "If anything, the only criticisms I got were to make it even more so. Occasionally the timer bothers someone, but usually they all agree that it's a good idea, and they like knowing they'll get their time. The homework assignment, having to take some kind of step every week, is another part of it that people like."

For career counselors supervising new teams, or teaching the *Teamworks!* course:

An important part of team coaching is preparing your Success Teams to be self-sustaining (unless your team members signed up for a semester course, or unless an ongoing team chooses to hire you to stay on as leader). Here's how to do it:

—From the beginning, impart not just the Success Team's content—dreams, goals, obstacles, brainstorming, etc.— but also its structure: time rules, clock timer, homework.

—Empower team members by encouraging them to be aware of their own skills and resources. "One thing I'm very interested in doing for people is getting them to realize that they know a whole lot," says Melanie Keveles, who works with displaced homemakers. "I don't have all the ideas. I'm very interested in not promoting myself as the expert."

—When I ran the fourteen-week course, I told my group in advance that I'd only be there for eight of those sessions, and I wasn't going to tell them which ones (I chose my six absences from weeks four through twelve)—for exactly the reasons we've been talking about. This gave me time to troubleshoot any problems when I came back. I was deliberately absent three times in a row toward the end. When I returned, the members had really taken over and didn't *want* a leader anymore. If that hadn't been the case I'd have devoted one meeting to making them more skilled at troubleshooting.

—Sending your teams out on their own doesn't mean you can't continue to give them support and access to resources. Each Success Team you graduate can become a part of your creative community. Invite teams to take part in a monthly networking meeting (see p. 66). Or offer to make a return visit in two months or so, for an update on team members' progress (success stories for your newsletter!) and any troubleshooting that's needed.

By using these guidelines, Success Teams can have the best

of both worlds—the clarity and momentum that comes from leadership, and the egalitarian self-reliance of a team of peers.

6. Bringing emotional problems to Success Team meetings. Hayward, California, jewelry designer Christofer A. said that one of the teams she led ran into trouble when "very personal and intense counseling type problems started coming up in sessions." A major contributing factor to that team's demise was members "bringing inappropriate issues to the group, ones that required professional counseling skills or qualifications to handle and were not within my scope of expertise."

On the other hand, Somerville, Massachusetts, actor/director Derek C. reports that for his team, honestly sharing emotional issues has been inseparable from making progress toward goals. "These are people that you get to trust after a while," he says. "We'd talk about the issues that were coming up in our own lives, and how we might work on them or function with them, and a mixture of hidden psychological issues and problems started to emerge, as well as dealing with the practical problems. We started to become a kind of mutual support group, and we were able to work our way through some of the concerns that had been stopping us from doing what we felt we could do. We've become very fast friends as a result, as well as making some significant life changes and choices." So, far from sinking this team, the mutual baring of souls had bonded it.

Who's right? How much "psychological stuff" can, or should, a Success Team handle? Where do you draw the line between mutual support and group therapy? What should your team do if one of its members is seriously troubled?

Remember, first of all, that the goal of a Success Team is for each of its members to reach his or her goal. The team's focus is strategy and action, not analysis, sympathy, or consciousness-raising. Note that the *Teamworks!* techniques for dealing with down moods and fear—hard times and intensive care—do not ask why the team member is feeling that emotion. They accept the fact that the emotion is natural, and deal with it in a brisk, practical, good-humored way that enables the person to start moving again.

That said, a Success Team can't completely shut out its members' personal and emotional lives. It's a fact that intense feelings do sometimes arise in the process of rediscovering and going for what we want. Past disappointment and anger may be wrapped around our dreams. A Success Team can become "a supplementary family," in Laurie Z.'s words, "where we're trying to get the encouragement that most of us didn't have when we were growing up." The experience of getting real support may release painful memories if our first family failed us.

Then, too, not all our goals will be coolly career-oriented. Some of the most important things we want are emotional: to find a romantic partner; to save or end a troubled marriage; to deal with a difficult friend or relative; to become less shy or more assertive. The question is how a Success Team can handle these issues without getting bogged down in confessions and obsessions—or straying into risky regions that require professional skill.

The answer is, you treat emotional problems as strategic problems. No matter what anyone brings in to the team—"I need a pair of shoes," "I'm having a nervous breakdown," "My husband's leaving me," "I have to find a green llama by Wednesday"—you simply respond with "What do you want?" and "What's the problem?" For example, if someone comes to a team meeting and says "My marriage is in trouble," the team doesn't say, "Poor kid. Tell us all about it." You're working within a time limit, remember, and the person's best use of team time is *not* just to unburden himself or herself. This is an action group. Empathy here gets expressed as strategy. So you listen for a few minutes, and then you ask three questions:

—"What do you want to do about it?"
—"What's stopping you?"
   and
—"How can we help?"

If the person says, "I want to hang on to my marriage, but my husband is talking about leaving," you say, "Okay, do you want to brainstorm that? Or shall we help you find a good marriage counselor?" Whenever a problem arises that is clearly beyond the team's competence, it's the Success Team's job to direct the team member to a good source of professional help: a therapist, marriage counselor, lawyer, or mediator (or a plumber or electrician, for that matter). That not only takes good care of your teammate, it also protects your team by restricting its focus to the things it does best.

What your team does best will depend on the inclinations of its members. Some teams choose to focus exclusively on career, while others freely mix the personal and the professional. If team members prefer that kind of mix, there's only one other criterion for whether or not it's working: forward motion. Are team members getting somewhere in their lives? Is everyone getting their full share of team help at every session? Or is the team turning into a true-confessions group or a gripe group, an excuse to stay stuck?

It's surprising how many personal problems can be handled by a combination of strategy and support. Your Success Team can sometimes help you resolve a sticky issue with your spouse—by brainstorming the smartest way to bring the issue up, rehearsing you, and then giving you the courage to actually do it. (Lucy F.'s team helped one teammate initiate financial discussions with her new husband.) The team can help you design and then stick to any kind of self-enhancement program, from diet and exercise to meditation, personal growth, or continuing education. (Julie D. of Albuquerque told of a professionally successful teammate who, with her team's help, designed a strategy for personal change: "What she wanted was to become more spontaneous and expressive—more outrageous! So she's taking acting classes, and it's helping.") Your team can even help you find a date or a mate (for some inspiration on that one, see Boy (Girl) Scouts of America, p. 211, and The White Elephant Sale, p. 213).

A Success Team is for finally getting unstuck in all those places in your life where the highest barriers have confronted the strongest longing—whether you define them as professional or personal.

7. Team member on strike! Occasionally it may happen that someone in your team won't do any homework for week after week after week. This could be for one of several reasons:

She is between goals. "One of my teammates finally had her dream job that she'd pushed so hard for, so then she lost her momentum," Marcia J. recalled. After reaching a major goal, you need time to sit and look at what you've done. "Sometimes people come to a point where they say, 'You know, I don't have a goal this week,' " says Lucy F. "It may be that they just need to stop before coming up with a new focus." It's okay not to have a goal for a while; a member gets and gives valuable energy just by being in the team and supporting the others. But if someone goes on for several weeks without a goal, it's time to check it out carefully.

There is a personal crisis. When a team member has a family problem—an illness, death, divorce, trouble with a child—he may need to temporarily suspend work on personal goals, and set a short-term goal of simply coping with the daily demands of the crisis. The team can shift to supporting the member in coping, finding help, and doing what needs to be done. But the team also acts as the guardian of the dream the member has put on hold—a precious reminder that there will be personal rewards beyond the crisis.

Wrong goal. A member's noticeable lack of enthusiasm for the steps she's agreed to take can be a signal that she is on the wrong track. We can't be completely sure that we'll love a certain path till we've had a taste of it. Someone who thought she'd like being a newspaper reporter might start doing research and be appalled by the hours real reporters work and the pressures on them. Our fathers taught us to finish what we start, but I emphatically disagree if you find you've started the wrong thing.

This is a little tricky, though, because terror can masquerade as indifference. Before someone switches goals, make sure she isn't still in love with the first one. She might just be facing something hard to do and getting cold feet. "If we could wave a magic wand and give it to you, would you still want it?" If the answer is no, don't waste another moment. Change.

Rebel on the loose. Every once in a while, a team member will simply say, "Guess what I did last week? Nothing. Guess what my problem is? Nothing. Guess what I'm gonna do next week? Nothing. I'm digging in my heels." Then you say, "Fine! Next." "Sometimes we needed permission from each other to relax and take a break—to not do it this week," says artist Karen R.

People have their own rhythms. They cannot be forced. When they see everyone else in the team making progress, they'll get back in the mood. Cheerful patience with a striking member almost always results in either laughter and release, or a revelation of the real fear behind the block, which can be handled by brainstorming (does this person need more information? preparation? rehearsal?) or by intensive care.

Occasionally, a team member will find life change too threatening, despite all the team's support, and will drop out just at the point when things are starting to move for him or her. "The main problem was she needed to take control of her life and not leave it in the hands of others, parents and husband," an Illinois teamworker recalls of one teammate. "She needed a great deal of support to do this. However, she withdrew first from the group because of these problems and never really addressed the issues again with the group." A Success Team can't "*make* someone do what she wants to do" if that person isn't yet ready for change. The less judgmental the team is at that point, the easier it is for the team member to come back at a later date. Often that person knows best, and should be trusted.

THE NATURAL LIFESPAN OF A SUCCESS TEAM

There you have them: the seven most common problems that plague Success Teams. Handle them wisely, and your team should have a long and fruitful life. But what does "long" mean, anyway? What's the natural lifespan of a Success Team? Is there an optimum amount of time to stay together to do all team members the most good? Can Success Teams keep meeting indefinitely?

In theory, why not? In practice, only a few teams have met formally for more than about two years. However, I know of a wonderful *eight*-year team in Minneapolis! The mobility and busyness of all our lives usually gives teams a considerably shorter lifespan. But what often ends a good Success Team is its success. The member who dreamed of moving to Australia moves to Australia. The member who wanted a job in Boston is now ensconced in Boston. Everyone else is engrossed in doing what she or he loves, and has less time and less need for the mutual support of the team.

So while there's no real reason why a Success Team couldn't go on for years, it usually turns out to be an intensive, time-limited process—but one that transforms your life for good. Being in a team changes you in two important ways:

—by vastly expanding your sense of what is possible, and
—by convincing you of your need for—and your right to—support.

Once you've broken through the barriers of ignorance, fear and inertia, it gets easier to do it the next time, and the next time. Those barriers don't look so high anymore, and you don't need so much tender loving care to coax you past them every time. On the other hand, you know how to recognize when you do need support, and you know how to get it: create and run a new Success Team, or create an informal support network for yourself.

Virginia C. was just coming out of a divorce when her Success Team began meeting in 1976. "I'd never had to support myself and my children. I had always worked, but never with that feeling that I had to earn a particular amount of money. Now, bang—I suddenly had to." By the time her team stopped meeting formally two years later, Virginia had not only established a successful business as a medical illustrator, she'd bought her own two-and-a-half-acre minifarm in upstate New York. "I was very specific in what I wanted: a house, a barn, a creek, for not more than $25,000. I couldn't afford any more. Everybody had said, 'You'll never find it'—except my team. Well, I found it! It was a handyman's special, and it's taken six or seven years to get it all fixed up. I've renovated the barn, too, and I have probably the world's most beautiful studio, with four door-sized windows overlooking that creek. After I bought it, my team came up and spent a weekend, and we had one of our meetings in a field, with sheep grazing nearby! The team idea is so good, because making those kinds of decisions alone is very frightening. To have somebody else, even if they're scared too, just makes it easier.

"Now I have a new goal, and I could use a team again. I want to spend more time with my own painting and drawing. My children are out of college, or almost, and I have a new freedom. But I'd need a lot of support, because while my ego is just fine as a medical illustrator, it's lousy as a painter. I'm so vulnerable in that regard.

"I'll probably call the teammate I've stayed in closest touch with, and talk to her about it. I'm also building up a group of artists, both upstate and here, who I can talk with about these feelings, so that they aren't quite so hidden or secret. I have a writer friend who I'm in touch with a great deal, and there are a couple of painters here in Brooklyn that I admire tremendously and talk with and trust. And I can also turn around and do the same thing for them. It's an informal equivalent of the team."

The team process is so powerful that even teams that don't last very long have a permanent impact on their members' lives. Marlissa M., whose team "died an untimely death" soon after the departure of its leader, said that "it completely transformed some people. We were so amazed at some of the things that happened"—such as Annemarie P.'s dramatic discovery of the place where she wanted to live (p. 129). "I moved here from California shortly before the group started, and the group was like an instant family for me. It meant everything to have their support," said Marlissa.

"A lot started for me" said Marcia J., another member, who worked for an airline but wanted to move into the arts. "Finally I really found goals and was able to tell the goals to people, and to draw up a plan. I took a class on how to be in commercials, I started doing some more writing for work, and just recently I started an internship at one of the cable TV shows. That was a direct result of finally being able to define where I wanted to go. It was really a wonderful experience for me." That team lasted five and a half months.

Circumstances and chemistry help decide the lifespan of a team. Even if you do everything right, I can't promise you that your team will live forever—or even for two years. But it will almost certainly change your life.

14...

Success Stories

The annals of team history are packed with stories of people who've done things, thanks to their Success Teams, that they'd never been able to do before: buy a house, start a business, change careers, write a book. When we began to pull together material for *Teamworks!*, I put the call out to all the Success Teams who'd written through the years and asked them for some updates on their members. I got a flood of phone calls and letters, packed with success stories, large and small. You've read many of these stories throughout this book, as illustrations of the way Success Teams work. But I can't resist telling you a few more—or letting team members tell you, in their own words.

Some team participants had completely overhauled their lives. Samantha, for instance. "I admired Samantha the most because she was so very determined," writes her teammate, jewelry designer Christofer ("Kit") A. of Hayward, California. "When she came to the group, she was extremely unhappy with both her personal and work situations. She was working as a secretary/clerk in a local hospital and absolutely hated it." Samantha's team encouraged her to find something she'd like better, and after some deliberation, Kit writes, "she devised the goal of making a complete change in her life: She decided she wanted to live and work in Australia!"

Team meeting by team meeting, Samantha methodically made her plans. "The entire group watched in awe as she sold all her household goods, stored whatever was left, and made all her arrangements (travel, visa, etc.) to move to Australia. We all went to the San Francisco airport in January of 1986 (right on Samantha's schedule—she wanted to see the Australia's Cup that month) to see her off . . . Though Samantha went through many, many trials and tribulations over the next year and a half, I recently heard from her, and she reported the following: in September of 1987, Samantha married an Australian man she met through placing an ad. She'd answered *his* ad in the same paper requesting the same thing—marriage!"

If the Samanthas among us need to launch a life's adventure, sometimes weary adventurers need to settle down. Rebecca S. came into her team with a master's degree in international affairs, years of experience working in Germany with a radio station, and other credits her team thought were very glamorous. Now she'd been back in the States for two years, and she was really lost. She had no idea what to do with herself and wasn't in the mood for Europe or glamour anymore. She was working as an underpaid drudge in an office, and hated it. Her teammate Harvey F. tells how Rebecca found her new direction:

"We questioned her week after week, and anytime she showed the slightest interest in something, we'd try to get her a day in the field, that is, a chance to visit somebody who was doing it. (She's a talented dress designer and seamstress, for one thing, and we managed to get her a day inside a very good fashion house.)

"But Rebecca was really dislocated after being out of the country for so long, and had a hard time finding something she could believe in. Then one day it came to her. She was actually a little hesitant to tell us because it seemed so very unglamorous and three of us are artists: she wanted to learn accounting and make a living as a financial planner. We were so happy she'd found something she wanted that we overlooked our horror of numbers and backed her up all the way. She was so delighted by our enthusiasm that she tracked down a good school, and even changed to a much better job. She worked on that CPA for three years. It seemed so hard to us, going to school after work almost every night. We asked her how the devil she did it, and I'll never forget the look on her face when she turned to us and said, "But I'm good at it." She was lit up. Her grades were sensational. She actually liked that hard work! She expects to have her CPA within the year. Her teacher has already lined her up with a first-rate company. I guess you really know down deep what's right for you."

And then there was Virginia C.'s teammate, a weary social-service worker who, with her team's support, found the energy to make a spectacular career change. "She'd been working in the hospital system with mentally retarded children, and she was burned out. She told us she wanted to do something entirely different. She didn't know what—except that she knew she wanted to make a lot of money." The social worker's teammates asked her to fantasize her ideal day. The results were startling: "She wanted to be a snappy executive and live in a loft in SoHo and really have the Life!"

The team brainstormed with her about what field to go into. "She decided to go into radio advertising, and she did it. Did she ever do it! She jumped from a salary of $15,000 a year to $60,000, then $75,000, then— We'd come into the meeting just a few months later and she'd be showing us her latest beautiful leather boots or fur coat, and the latest changes that were made in the loft. I mean, it was *dramatic!*" After fully enjoying her success and her new lifestyle, the social worker–turned–executive was ready for another change: she became a mother, and stayed happily at home with her baby for a while.

If a superwoman executive sometimes lurks under a social worker's modest jacket, it's as often true that a high-powered executive longs to do something just for love, not for profit. A well-paid professional can feel every bit as trapped in his or her job and role as a hospital orderly or a computer operator. And, since society offers little encouragement for such "impractical" moves, it often takes a Success Team to blast her loose—by nurturing belief in the need and the right to do what she really loves (that *is* success!), and supporting the move every step of the way.

Rob was a successful forty-four-year-old liaison and public-relations officer with a national organization of paper mills. He was happily married and lived, when he wasn't flying between meetings, with his wife and high-school age children in a beautiful home in Illinois. On a plane one day, looking through the airlines magazine, he saw a picture of a man a few years older than himself, dressed in khaki pants and shirt, smiling happily, one foot up on a jeep running board, a large, black crow standing on the other. The man was the chief ranger for a wildlife preserve in Wyoming. Rob sighed deeply. On his vacation he wouldn't even get to visit such a place, because he wanted to be with his family, and they liked to go to Florida. Well, he rationalized, you probably have to go back to school and get a degree in something for that; I have no right to complain. Life's been good to me. Can't have everything. Still, when his eye wandered back to that picture, he became a little sad.

I was Rob's first Success Team. I was on that plane with him, and I listened to his dream of being a wildlife ranger and his list of insurmountable difficulties with the kind of objective ear a teammate can offer. "Why," I wondered, "would you need a degree in anything? A man like the one in that magazine must have access to all the degreed employees he needs. Maybe what he needs is a veteran businessman who flies around the country for a living. Why don't you contact that man personally and talk to him?" Rob got as shy and uncertain as a school kid. "Why would he want to talk to me?" he said. "I don't know, but I have a hunch that he would," I answered. "Do it. I dare you."

Six months later I received a photograph of the two of them standing next to each other in an open field, both wearing khaki pants and shirts, both smiling, and on the front, one word. "Thanks." It turned out that Rob got his family together to think things out, and when they saw how close to his heart this dream was, *they* became his Success Team. (See p. 187 for tips on turning your family into your team.) They came up with a great plan: get the paper mills interested in supporting wildlife preserves as a public-relations project—and start vacationing all together in Wyoming instead of Florida.

Other team members had taken what might look like a small step to someone else, but was a major breakthrough in terms of how they felt about themselves. Often, with the team's support, they dared to explore their creativity for the first time. "I feel I received the most from my team, focusing on what I want and taking a tiny step in the right direction," wrote Ronda H.

of Skokie, Illinois. "I realized I had to do something creative even though I'm terrified of criticism, and I would like to receive recognition for these accomplishments, which always seemed too self-centered to admit. In the fall of 1986 I took a creative writing course, enjoyed myself thoroughly and excelled in it at the same time!"

"Something totally new came up for one woman," writes team leader Julie Dunleavy of Albuquerque, New Mexico. "She's a social worker, and she discovered through her fantasies that she wanted to write. She hasn't gotten a lot written yet, but she discovered something that she never knew was there. It was a real 'aha' moment for her."

"There were many small victories, that were really major breakthroughs for the individual," said team leader LaVaun Maier of Milwaukie, Oregon. "D., a fifty year old, divorced woman, after painfully gathering up the bits and pieces of her life, discovered how to take charge and direct her own life. She began learning tap dancing—and invited us all to her first recital!" Another teammate, I., felt her useful life was over at age sixty-eight. The team encouraged her to discover and define the one thing that meant the most to her—the core theme of her life, her touchstone. "Finally identifying her touchstone— *to be needed*—inspired I. to apply for a new deaconess assignment with her church," wrote LaVaun. "A few months later, she had moved from the West Coast to the East Coast and begun a year-long assignment at a Lutheran Children's Home in New York!"

Our team chronicles overflow with stories about projects completed after years on the back burner, careers established after years of hesitation, and creative solutions found to the problem of financially supporting artistic work. "Mary had been working on her book for quite a while, but she just couldn't imagine that she could get it published," Julie Dunleavy wrote from Albuquerque. The team helped Mary carry out her plan for approaching publishers, and supported her in the difficult process of researching publishing houses, sending out query letters, and surviving rejections. The result: "She got a publisher interested, and she's doing a rewrite." Another team member, a sculptor, wanted to show on the East and West coasts and to appear in *Art in America*. "He came into the team feeling discouraged that it could ever happen," said Julie. "The team helped him articulate his goal, identify the steps to it, and believe it was possible. He's had several new galleries pick him up on both coasts, and his work has been prominently advertised in *Art in America*."

"I started out telling the team I wanted to marry a millionaire, who would support me in my life as a writer," Stella M. said over the phone from L.A. "In the course of the team meetings, I realized that that wasn't it. I just could not stand to go back to work for anybody, but I didn't want to have to struggle to make a living at writing, either. I needed to be economically independent to write. So my teammate Mary and I brainstormed, and we decided to open a resale retail shop—a warehouse outlet for rattan furniture and collectibles. We've rented the space, we've been spending fourteen hours a day getting it ready, and we'll open in a couple of weeks. I feel great about it. Being economically independent is the best thing that could happen to me."

"When our team started, I had just quit my last full-time legal secretarial job (which I loathed)," writes Kit A. "I had visions of taking the world by storm and being both a famous trainer/ motivational speaker *and* a sought-after jewelry designer. Needless to say, during the team sessions I began to see that I would have to choose, and I realized that one of the businesses was closer to my heart and soul than the other." She imagined an ideal life, to help her decide.

"My touchstone: I am a famous, wealthy designer/artist. My work is sought after and marketed worldwide." That did it. She realized how important being an artist was to her and gave it all her energy.

"In the last year, I have made tremendous strides toward the fulfillment of my touchstone, including becoming much more focused, more professional, and certainly more serious. I have exhibited at several shows, taken specialized sales training to accomplish the marketing of my work and services, and have already expanded my client base about twofold over last year. I see myself becoming ever more focused and centered on my goal, and I can't tell you how much happier I am than when I was a secretary. I know without a doubt that [the team] was the best investment I could have made in my own future!"

These stories show you what can happen to you, too, when you put yourself in the environment of your own Success Team. And if you are (or want to be) in the business of helping people, these stories are a sample of the small miracles that can happen for your clients when you get them into teams and empower them to help each other.

In the next chapter, I'm going to talk to career developers in independent practice, in corporations and colleges, outplacement and vocational rehabilitation, senior centers and retirement communities, about how they can put Success Teams to work for their clients. But if you're not one of those professionals—if you're a student, a retired person, unemployed, or feeling at a dead end in your job—don't go away! In these next pages there are ideas for you, too. Show this book to your teacher, guidance counselor, boss, or recreation director. Or take things into your own hands and start one of these specialized teams for yourself.

15...

Success Teams in the Helping Professions

Success Teams can work wonders in a wide variety of settings: from corporations to high school and college classrooms, from retirement communities to economically depressed communities where joblessness is epidemic. The way you'll use them differs a little bit depending on the population you work with. The following suggestions are keyed to professionals in specific fields:

If you are a human-resource manager or trainer-developer, you're working with people who've already had experience with teams and teamwork—but of a very different kind.

In a corporate team, all the members work together on a corporate goal: developing a new product, taking over a new market. The team serves the corporation. In a Success Team, all the members work together on their own personal goals—they serve each other. In case you're wondering how that could possibly be of any use to a corporation, I will give you two good reasons for putting your employees into special lunch-hour Success Teams I call Dream Teams. One is motivation and morale; the other is communications and team bonding.

1. *Motivation and morale.* One of the reasons I get called out to create Success Teams in some corporations is that although the companies are doing very well, there's not much upward mobility for most employees. There's some incentive that can be offered in terms of salary raises, but middle managers, secretaries, and production workers alike can feel that they're going nowhere. They may like their jobs, the company may have made them as comfortable as possible, but those jobs feel like dead ends, and in our culture, a dead end is like death. Americans need to be going somewhere. It's just the way we are.

Corporations don't want dissatisfied workers, but they can't keep giving promotions. Vacations often leave employees just as restless when they get back. A more promising strategy some companies have adopted is to offer self-enhancement options, such as health seminars or investment seminars or a beautiful gym to work out in. Companies that take an interest in the quality of their employees' lives are rewarded with better performance and higher productivity. Corporate Success Teams are my contribution to this type of incentive, and they are proving amazingly effective. One of the most powerful ways to improve the quality of a person's life is to ask, "What do you really want?" and then announce, "We're going to help you get it." But for effectiveness in a corporation, the standard Success Team design has to be modified a little bit.

The first time I taught Success Teams in a corporate setting, I was called out to do a seminar for a small, forward-looking electronics firm in Pennsylvania. The human-resource person who called me had been through my seminar, but I still thought I'd better warn him: "Bill, if you bring me in to run a seminar, you're taking two big risks. The first is that the people in the seminar will change careers and become poets and sky divers, and you'll be out of business. The second is that they'll reveal their ambitions within your company—like angling for your job—and you'll fire them."

He laughed. "No, I've already thought of that. Neither one of those things is going to happen. I have a plan. How would you like to come out here and launch people on their *personal* dreams?" And corporate "Dream Teams" were born.

Initiated at a lunch-hour seminar (like the one described on p. 90) and sustained in weekly lunchtime team meetings, Dream Teams are just like Success Teams, except that they're focused exclusively on personal, noncareer goals: to buy a house, to own a horse, to write a novel, to get married, to visit Hawaii, to get a child into medical school. Dream Teams are a powerful incentive program, one that pays off in increased employee satisfaction and productivity, because a worker who feels that her paycheck is allowing her to fulfill a personal dream doesn't have to demand the impossible from her job. Life comes to have excitement to it, and the job becomes a friend for supporting this exciting life.

2. *Communications and team bonding.* The *Wishcraft/Teamworks!* seminars and Dream Teams provide superb—and painless—training in communications and project management skills. Team members set personal goals such as "lose twenty pounds," "write five chapters," "get a home in the Bahamas." While having fun articulating their dreams and brainstorming the obstacles, they learn to listen to each other keenly, to speak in a highly focused way, and to plan projects and use time effectively—skills that will enhance their performance at work. Brainstorming personal goals stimulates creativity in a low-risk, noncompetitive setting that's the antithesis of the average corporate team. In fact, putting corporate teammates into Dream Teams can create trust and open communication—and better corporate team performance—in place of stress and alienation.

A typical corporate team is a team on the old masculine model of the high-school football team. How does the team's corporate coach provoke the aggressive spirit that seems necessary in the competitive business world, yet still bond group members together as a team? Often, he criticizes and rewards the members inside the team, so that they're competing with each other. (I have worked with corporations brainstorming development of new products, and whenever one person would come up with an idea everybody else tried their best to shoot it down. They seemed to think that was a good idea.) Then he might give them an outside enemy, so they're unified during the game. That approach used to be considered the only way to win in business. But opinions are changing. On closer examination, it's clear that team members were not thinking of ways to improve company performance, they were thinking, "What's the real hierarchy in this team? Whose toes will I step on if I'm too talkative? What if I come up with too many good ideas?" Everyone's goal was to survive inside the team, no longer to come up with the best material. Creativity was inhibited and morale was low.

So how do you get the members of a corporate team to trust each other and enjoy working together? For a time some corporations tried radical solutions. They put employees into T-groups and sensitivity trainings, explosive sessions where people were supposed to be emotionally honest. Often, that became another kind of tyranny. "Some people cried and admitted their alcoholism and their infidelities," one CEO told me. "It went much too far in the other direction. It ripped our unit apart." That's because a corporation is not a family. Too much closeness is as disruptive as too little.

There is a certain amount of intimacy that's just right in a corporate setting, and that's what Dream Teams create. You could call it light intimacy—the perfect middle ground between the open-your-soul style and the old political play-it-close-to-the-vest. In a Dream Team, I will never know if you're loaded with personal problems or not, and I don't want to know. What I will know is that you've always wanted your own horse, and your face lights up when you talk about it. That's the best part of people, anyway, at least the best you can know about people you hardly know: what they love and what they want. And it's something that everybody shares. Everybody has a secret dream, and when you hear what those dreams are, the right kind of friendship is established.

So when the woman in charge of graphics is in a team with the production manager, and she talks about how she's always wanted to sing, he might say, "Listen, my daughter wanted to sing. Let me tell you what she did." At the end of the meeting, when he says, "You go ahead and sing. You do it. I want to hear next week that you called that singing teacher," she really likes him. And that carries over into their work together. A Dream Team can be used as a warm-up team that creates an extraordinarily cooperative and effective corporate team.

The simplest way to start up Dream Teams in your company is for you, the human resource manager, to run your own version of the *Wishcraft/Teamworks!* short seminar (p. 81) in a conference room on site over a lunch hour. The small electronics company I mentioned earlier wanted employees to know how committed the company was to their satisfaction, and dem-

162 • • •

onstrated it by bringing me in for a full-day seminar broken up into two afternoon sessions of three hours each, a week apart. After that, I came back to oversee the first two regular Dream Team meetings. I ran only the first twenty minutes of the first meeting, coaching two people through their ten-minute process (What did you do last week? What problems can we brainstorm for you? What are your plans for next week?). I let them do the rest. And at the second meeting, I stayed in a corner of the room, available if needed.

As an in-house human-resources person, you can circulate among Dream Teams meeting weekly in the lunch room, keeping an eye on their progress and being available for troubleshooting. Every month or two, you can convene all teams for a large-group networking (p. 59), at which everyone from vice presidents to floor managers and typists report on their personal goals, their progress so far, and what they need to go further. It's like a mid-year Christmas party without the drinking, an excellent way to loosen the hierarchy and open up informal lines of communication in a company.

If you're interested in starting your own business as a career coach or *Wishcraft/Teamworks!* counselor, Success Teams are the key piece of the package of services I've been describing throughout this book. Just so you can find them again easily, the pieces of the package are:

—Your own resource bank, p. 42
—Network newsletter, p. 54
—Large-group brainstorming, p. 59
—The networking game, p. 64
—Monthly networking meetings, p. 66
—The *Wishcraft/Teamworks!* seminars, p. 78
—Success teams and team coaching, p. 143
—The buddy system, p. 182

To sum up: You can run several seminars a year for local organizations to build your reputation and your clientele. You can start up Success Teams at the end of each seminar, and coach them for six to eight meetings. You'll want to maintain your own resource bank, and offer individual goal counseling for private clients. In addition, you can invite all your team members and individual clients to come to monthly networking meetings, and/or to subscribe to a network newsletter full of brainstorming challenges and success stories.

I put this package together in response to the hundreds of people who have written to me saying, "I'd like to be doing what you're doing." It's my belief that people drawn to this kind of work have a talent for it, and I'd like to encourage them—and you—to pursue it. *Wishcraft/Teamworks!* counseling is a ready-made opportunity for any people-person who would like to be an independent entrepreneur in a service business. I especially recommend it to women who are just entering the work force, or leaving unchallenging jobs, and don't quite know what they're qualified to do. Most women are very skilled at this particular service; they do it effortlessly—because they've had so much experience. But more and more men are discovering a talent for it, too.

This business could be for you if:

—you want to be part of a network of creative, energetic people, all helping each other achieve their personal goals

—you're good at working with and helping people

—you want to be doing work that is exciting, truly worthwhile, and fun

—you want to be your own boss, and make money at it

—you want to be known and respected by the businesses and organizations in your area

—you have next to no start-up capital

—you don't want to pay sums or percentages of your business once you get it going, as franchisees do

As I've said, you're welcome to use the *Teamworks!* and *Wishcraft* names and material without getting my special permission. All I ask in return is that you share the books with your clients.

If you are a high school or college advisor, Success Teams can multiply your reach and impact, as well as relieve the loneliness and confusion of kids who face some terrifying decisions. Being in a team helps students feel more confident about their future, supports them in making some of the most important choices of their lives, and teaches them networking skills that they'll need after graduation.

"High school kids in teams definitely need adult supervision," says Nyack, New York, teacher Susan Hadley, who guides the Nyack Success Team, a group of twenty to twenty-five juniors, each semester at Nyack High School. "We've tried doing it both during the school day, in a forty-five-minute class, and after school. I find that it works much better after school, because we have more time. Eighteen to twenty of the kids complete the program successfully, which means coming every time." She also pairs students off with planning partners, who are responsible for reminding each other to do homework and come to meetings. "We have them set goals each week with their buddy. At the next meeting I'll say, 'How many people completed their goals? If you didn't, why not, and what can we do as a group to help you?' "

Though extracurricular, Sue's Success Team is essentially a semester course, meeting weekly for twelve weeks. "A lot of high school students need to build up their self-confidence and self-esteem, before they can come up with an answer to the question 'What would you really love to do?'" So Sue's students spend the first several weeks "doing research on themselves," using a combination of *Teamworks!* exercises, Richard Bolles's techniques from *What Color Is Your Parachute?*, and Sue's own inventions. "I set down very basic ground rules. You've got to have positive vibes in there—no put-downs are allowed. They need the supportive environment to be able to dream and risk talking about who they are. I work through a process where they examine what their skills are and what their values are. They love the Pick a Color exercise [p. 109]. They love Praise Behind Your Back [p. 111]. That's very good for building self-esteem. I have them tell stories of things they've done that they were proud of, using Your Magnificent Seven, an exercise from Bolles. Once students have a better sense of who they are, then they're freed up to think about what they'd love to do."

After researching themselves, the kids research the world of work to try to find a fit. "We cram a lot into just twelve weeks. One of the sessions is a field trip. We choose a place where there are lots of different jobs, so students can see a variety of possibilities. At the job site we divide them up into small groups, and they go talk to people in each of those jobs. For example, this year we took twenty-three kids on a field trip to IBM. They interviewed people in such jobs as field engineering, computer graphics, systems analysis, programming, and support services. They were all very high on it. And one hundred percent of our students find meaningful jobs using the skills they've learned."

The only problem with the Nyack Success Team, Sue says, is that it ends. "The kids develop a real sense of community, and I feel as bad as they do when it's over. We're starting to develop ongoing support groups for Success Team 'graduates.' And I'm doing teacher training to incorporate the Success Team materials and methods into their classrooms. Funding is the hard part, with all the budget cutbacks."

More good ideas for high school Success Teams:

—Show kids that they have a potential network in their own and each other's parents and relatives, their teachers, neighbors, and community businesspeople. High school students might not have many resources of their own to exchange, at least not for pursuing career goals, but there are adults in their lives who do. Sue Hadley tells success team members, "List twenty people you know. That's your network!"

—Kids, like the rest of us, can get stopped by negative feelings. To let them know that these feelings are natural, use Hard Times [p. 93 and 131] for unpleasant tasks like homework ("Put it on the floor, stomp on it, curse it, and then sit down and start. You don't have to like it, you just have to do it!") and Intensive Care [p. 132] for intimidating ones such as interviews. Young people need to experience pushing through an obstacle to the feelings of relief and triumph on the other side.

High school and college teachers and counselors can make good use of the *Teamworks!* course plan on p. 94. It starts with team-building, guides students through self-exploratory exercises from *Wishcraft*, and then settles into a weekly Success Team meeting.

If you're in the career development office of a college or

university, Success Teams can help you serve both students and alumni. Most college career counselors I've talked to have two complaints: "Not enough students use our services," and "If they did, we couldn't handle them all." Run a short seminar (one to two hours is best), start teams, and you can attract and accommodate a large number of people. Students will be able to have an ongoing support system while they're in school. Success Teams can break down the isolation that makes undergraduate problems loom so large, and offer freshmen a way to move into the college culture right from the start. Sophomore teammates help each other pick their majors and stay on top of studies and papers; juniors and seniors use teams to start job-searching and preparing for being out in the world. Best of all, the groundwork is laid for a network of helping hands after graduation. Students need all these kinds of support, but will rarely come to the guidance office to ask for them.

I did a seminar once for students at a major graduate business school. They were utterly silent through the whole presentation; nobody laughed. I thought I'd missed the boat with them. Hours later I went outside and saw them standing around under trees in little circles, still talking! Their evaluation sheets gave the seminar a top grade. It turned out that many of them weren't sure they wanted to be in business at all! They were afraid to tell anybody, because they were already committed to a prestigious business school, surrounded by the go-for-the-gold gang, and their parents were paying a fortune in tuition. They didn't know that forty-two percent of the other kids in their class felt exactly the same way. Once they started talking to each other, they began to realize that they could either find wonderful aspects of business that they hadn't known existed, or they could get out of business and use their new skills in other ways. When the isolation ended, the progress began.

After graduation, every school likes to try to provide a network for alumni through the career office, but it's hard to track people down and to get a high response to mailings and questionnaires. To increase participation and enthusiasm, try running a short seminar (p. 81) or just a Networking Game (p. 64) at class reunions.

You'll find that the Networking Game becomes the most popular event at reunions. It's not passive, like listening to a speech, or impersonal like a visit to the career office to see how many contacts come up on the computer. It isn't an old-style networking cocktail party, where everybody stands around with a glass and a napkin trying to figure out how to use each other. It's a *game*. That's why everyone seems to like it. When they race around asking each other for things, everybody has fun and is in the mood to give, to help people out. Old boys' networks can get a little old, but this never loses its freshness. The Networking Game generates energy. Any alumni association that's done it once wants to run it every year, and even more often for locally based alumni. Participants from the same town can go home and run their own Success Teams, and everybody can sign up for a Network Newsletter (see p. 54) full of requests and resources, put out by the career office.

If you work in outplacement or vocational rehabilitation, where burnout and a high failure rate are occupational hazards, Success Teams could be a lifesaver for you—and for your clients as well. Here's why.

Often, the people you work with in this branch of counseling are at rock bottom. They've just been dumped out of a job they thought was theirs for life, or they're women in their middle years who have suddenly been plunged into the work force by divorce, widowhood, or a husband's illness. Your clients may be on welfare and unable to get off it; they may be chronic alcoholics or addicts, or homeless people caught in the vicious cycle of "Can't get a job without a home—can't get a home without a job." Or perhaps you work with veterans who lost a piece of themselves in Vietnam and have suffered too much rejection. People in these situations are demoralized, often angry, and they don't believe for a minute that wishes can come true. This is the population that can exhaust you with their resistance.

Hurt people are like drowning swimmers. They can pull you under without meaning to. You can wear yourself out just trying to get them to believe it's possible to get a résumé together, get dressed up, and go out and get a job. Every time you come up with a suggestion, they can look at you and say, "That won't work. I tried that. I can't." You may say, "Bring in the want ads and we'll go through them together," and they just shrug. If you're not careful, you find yourself becoming a human heart-and-lung machine, administering the oxygen of hope to the hopeless. After twenty years as a therapist and ten years of career counseling, I'm convinced that one of the major causes of professional burnout is simply that we're trying too hard to get sad people to be happy.

Brief seminars for group outplacement may not put as much stress on the career counselor, but I don't think they do much for the newly unemployed. A major corporation can lay off thousands of people in a day. Trying to help them get new jobs, they often put them into an impersonal three-day seminar that tells these shocked survivors how to dress for success and write a résumé—and that's it. Imagine if that were a Success Teams seminar instead. It would save the corporation a lot of money, and it would put those people into an ongoing support system—one that works far better than any high-priced, high-powered three-day blitz.

Here is a mystery. How can people too demoralized to help themselves actually succeed in helping each other? That's the alchemy of Success Teams. There are quite a few things down-in-the-dumps teammates can do for each other—with your guidance—that you alone can't do for them:

*Surround demoralized people with others like themselves, so they don't feel as if there's something wrong with them. When a team like this first starts, someone often says, "This process won't work. Who are you kidding? I'll never get a job." The others in the group may agree at once. Immediately there's relief and fellowship. They aren't alone with some Pollyanna social worker who's saying, "Don't worry! Everything will be fine!" They're with people who understand. You might think this would reinforce their negativity. Quite the contrary. The rapport and energy born of complaining together are what's going to carry this team to success.

*Turn losers into helpers—and build self-esteem while taking the load off the counselor. Team members may be too discouraged at first to make a move for themselves. That's all right. Encourage them to give ideas and support to the others. When a person is at a total loss, it's much easier to help a teammate, and that way he'll gain a new sense of value. If he says, "I know where you can find a used truck transmission. If you want, I'll take you there," suddenly he's not just a needy victim. He has something to give, and that gives him pride and power.

And it gives you, the career counselor, a break. You just stand outside the group and let it run, with only the most light-handed facilitation. No longer are you single-handedly trying to resurrect people whose hearts are broken. They're doing the job, and they are the ones who should be doing it, because they're the ones who need to do it for each other. It's a kind of therapy, and it works wonders.

Besides, you can't possibly give any one of them as much assistance as the team can. You're just one person handling five people, while each one of them has four others to call on. They can call each other ten times a week if they like. It lightens your load while giving them much more help than they'd get from you alone.

Jane Shuman of Springfield, Illinois, provided a concrete example of how Success Team members can support each other through what is usually a very lonely and frightening life passage. The programs for displaced homemakers in her state are designed to help homebound women who are trying to get back into the job market. "Most programs have components in self-esteem building and confidence-building, and components of trying to help people figure out what they want to do. I'm recommending using Success Teams from the very beginning of the process, to provide structure and support. If you're on this team because you want a job, that becomes the goal of everybody. There are certain tasks that need to be done to get that job that are much easier to do in a team than alone. For instance, during the component where they're going out and beginning information interviewing (a Bolles concept), they go out in twos instead of going alone. Then you make a list of everybody you know—become aware of your contact list, your network—and you need to be able to call all those people and let them know what kind of job you're looking for." Team members support each other through all the networking phone calls, the resulting interviews, and the almost inevitable disappointments along the road to success in finding a job.

*Surround nonmovers with buddies starting to move—and start to revive belief. Suppose five or six people are sitting in the meeting, feeling down, and another teammate comes in who couldn't even get his good shirt out of the cleaner's when the team started. Suddenly everyone notices that today he has his clean shirt on. He says with a kind of wonder, "I went to an appointment. I can't believe it. Joe and I rehearsed it, he got me ready, and I went. I don't know if I got the job, I don't think they were hiring"—but it doesn't matter, because everybody in the group knows what it means that he went for a job interview. All of a sudden, the other team members start thinking, "Wait a minute. If he can do it, maybe it's not impossible." Seeing is believing, and one example is far more powerful than any number of words from the counselor.

The problem with a demoralized person is that her belief mechanism is broken. If someone tells her she can get a job, she thinks, "There are no jobs out there. The want ads don't mean anything." In this state of mind, a person has only one belief left, and that is: "Nothing works." She will not be able to endure a single disappointment, because it will be all the proof she needs that she was right. People who still believe that things work, by contrast, can handle the number of disappointments that it always takes to get a yes.

You can't talk a demoralized person into believing. But if she sits there—in voc-rehab Success Teams, people are allowed to sit and not move for as long as they like—and sees a teammate accomplish one thing, just one small triumph, and that person has no more going for him than she does, then she can start to believe again. And with belief come the beginnings of energy and enthusiasm.

*Raise morale once every week. Your clients can stay demoralized all week, but once every week, something happens to raise their spirits: companionship, support, and movement. It's a change people learn to look forward to—a regular reminder that there's another way to feel about the world.

*Create an accountability system. One team member walks in, and everybody else wants to know what she did last week. "Did you make that call?" They really want to know. If she didn't call, nobody's going to hit her, or flunk her. This isn't an authoritarian system, like school, so there's no need to react with defiance. Team members just look disappointed. She realizes that she's let them down—not by failing to do something for them, but by failing to do something for herself. Someone cares enough to be reproachful that she didn't take better care of herself! It makes her feel responsible—and valued. She'd hate to disappoint them again.

*Create a cheering section—just some buddies to applaud and say, "You did it!" and clap their teammate on the back and make him feel proud of himself for each small step, so that he has the energy for the next one. It takes a team to do that. Because if he goes home and tells a tired or worried wife, "I bought the want ads!" she may say, "Oh? Will that pay the rent?" and there goes his winning streak. Somebody who isn't depending on him has to know what it means that he bought the want ads. And his teammates know, because they've been there.

A Success Team in outplacement or voc-rehab is frequently not a fireball of a Success Team. It doesn't move like the Indy 500. But it moves, and that's the whole point.

Lorna Hecker of Carbondale, Illinois, who is now studying for her Ph.D., tells how teams brought success to an area of very high unemployment in southern Illinois:

"In 1986 I was the counselor to a Single Parents and Home-makers Assistance Program at the McDonough County Rehabilitation Center, in Macomb, Illinois. At the onset of this program, I set up Success Teams with our new members. We coupled the Success Teams with job seeking skills, and we also had grant money for the women to have a day in the beauty salon, increasing their appearance skills. This, too, was an excellent self-concept builder. One woman said to me that she hadn't had her hair done since 1982.

"One of the special concerns I found in working with Single Parents was the low socioeconomic status. Because of this, I had to change the focus from future to present goals. While the financially solvent mothers were able to dream about future goals, the poor mothers could not seem to do that. How can a poor mother think about dreams for tomorrow when she is worried about finding enough formula to feed her baby today? These women can't achieve until they have even more basic needs met such as food and shelter.

"I dealt with this challenge by 1) focusing more on day-to-day goals, and 2) utilizing the networking session to hook these mothers up to the available social services where they could obtain some relief. Sometimes I had to stop focusing on the future and listen to the present pain. It seemed the women with emotional difficulties as well, e.g. depression, also had a difficult time planning for the future. I dealt with these aspects by breaking down the goals into very digestible and attainable goals, which seemed like molehills from my perspective, but mountains from theirs. I also found that respect for a person, no matter who they are, will help them believe in themselves, despite the poor situation they may be in. The single parents and homemakers I worked with were the most determined group of women I had ever met. Many of our women graduated from our local college and/or got good jobs. They were a joy to work with."

To work with people who need a job, rather than a career, doesn't mean that the career counselor has to leave his or her creativity at home. On the contrary, here's where imagination can really turn a dreary trudge through the slave market into a treasure hunt. One reason why the standard job hunt is so depressing and discouraging is that it doesn't connect with the "unique dimensions" of the person hunting, in the words of Duluth, Minnesota career counselor Melanie R. Keveles. Melanie views unemployment less as a catastrophe than as an opportunity to find work that really fits you. "I've loved working in the field of outplacement, or with displaced homemakers, or anybody in those populations," she says. "It's a challenge to brainstorm and to see how many different things you can come up with that you hadn't thought of before."

In FIRED for Success, an unconventional outplacement manual she wrote with her St. Louis partner Judith Dubin, Melanie dared to suggest to the stunned victims of layoffs that, "It may be the best thing that ever happened to you." "In my experience, people who get fired are generally unhappy with what they're doing," she says. "At some level, they've already made an unconscious decision to shut off. Maybe they loved the job five years ago, or maybe they love the security—I call it the golden handcuffs: 'How could I leave this job? I'm making good money. I have all these benefits.' But you sit with that person for an hour or so, and you find out that for the last three years they've been dying inside. So while on the face of it they have nothing to do with getting fired, they're actually more in control of the situation than they think.

"In our outplacement groups, instead of saying, 'Get them another job similar to the last one!' we'd essentially try to help people brainstorm about what they're all about, get in touch with what they really love, and begin to figure out ways in which they can do *that* for a living." Another controversial feature of Melanie and Judith's outplacement teams: "Instead of having the vice presidents in one group and the secretaries in another, we'd try to mix them together, because the secretaries have ideas for the VPs, and vice versa."

Melanie now uses a similar approach at Project Soar, a state and federally funded program for displaced homemakers in Duluth, Minnesota. "The area is very depressed. Duluth was a good nineteenth-century town, but the shipping has slowed down considerably from what it used to be, the mines have closed, and it's had an impact. There's been a lot of divorce. Douglas County across the water in Superior, where I live, has the second highest alcoholism rate in this country. A lot of wife-battering goes on, and as a consequence, some of the women just say *Enough.* And they qualify as displaced homemakers. They usually have several children. And it's 'Now what? What is there for me?' A good portion of them are on welfare, and they're not happy about that, but if they were to go out and get a minimum-wage job, they would lose their medical benefits. It's a crazy system.

"So what I do is try to instill hope, to get them thinking along the lines that maybe there's a possibility that they could actually do something they *enjoy.* Try to be as creative as possible about it." In front of the team, Melanie asks each participant goal-search questions (p. 36) such as, "What do you do like breathing?" "What did you love to do as a child?" "Is there somebody doing something that you really admire?" "Look at the way you've decorated your apartment. What does that say about you?" "It's the first time that they've ever encountered questions like that," she says. "Everybody else gives them these tests that tell them what they're supposed to do, and it's usually something they don't want to do at all! So they answer the questions in front of the group, and we write down all the different pieces of information, and then we brainstorm as a group: What could this person do?"

Sometimes, the answer is a bold departure from the clerical, sales, and hospital jobs that displaced homemakers traditionally fill. One of Melanie's clients, whose past work experience was secretarial, is launching a newspaper column on the outdoors. Jo Ann McGaw, a Seattle career counselor using a similar approach, teaches low-income women entrepreneurial skills. But it isn't the pursuit of a glamour job that makes the team goal-search process exciting. It's getting to know and value oneself, and choosing a job—even an ordinary job—that *fits*.

"I had a woman in one of these groups who had absolutely never done anything, ever," says Melanie Keveles. "And we were writing a résumé. So I said, 'Did you ever organize your drawers?' She said, 'Well, as a matter of fact, I did.' 'Did you ever do that for neighbors?' She said, 'Yes, actually, I did!' It turned out she'd done other kinds of organizing as well. So we put her organizing skills and experience on her résumé, and she was so excited when she saw it, because it said that she was worthy of doing something. She had some physical ailments, and decided that she wanted to get a job filing, because it wouldn't be too strenuous. She hadn't had any filing experience, but this at least showed that she had the capability." Another woman who'd collected rare teddy bears as a child decided to look for a job tracing lost items. (Melanie's teams meet for six weeks; then members pair off and are taught to exchange ongoing support using the buddy system—p. 182.)

If you work with people who are down on their luck, and you've given so many morale transfusions that you're anemic, try Success Teams. They release the human resources—the imagination, hope, and helpfulness—hidden in your clients themselves.

If you work with retired people, you know your clients have untapped inner riches: experience, talent, memory, and wisdom, and also wonder and imagination. Your challenge is to awaken and engage those inner resources so that retirement can be a time of exploration, fulfillment, and growth. You've got some handicaps to work against. Many older people have physical limitations, and many—cut off from work and family, losing old friends, living on strictly limited means—are lonely, frightened, or bitter. Our society tells old people in a thousand ways that they're unwanted and useless, that their productive, attractive years are over and all they can do now is wait to die. Yet with healthier lifestyles and medical advances, more and more of us are living into this life stage. It's time for a revolution in the way we live our old age, and Success Teams can be part of that revolution.

Success, for an older person, will mean something very different than it did to that same person in his or her twenties or forties. While physically and materially, age is a time of increasing limitation, mentally and spiritually it can be a time of liberation. In mid-life, we carry the world on our shoulders, taking care of growing kids and aging parents while meeting the peak demands of jobs or careers. We do feel involved and needed, but we don't have much time for ourselves, our dreams and wonderings, the things we've always wanted to learn, the hobbies we've put aside. When old age comes, we've earned a freedom from responsibility not so different from that of a child, whose only job in life is to learn and play. As long as our physical needs are met, age is a fresh chance to learn about the stars, to try painting or potting or acting or playing the clarinet, to write short stories or tape our memories—to do some of the things we always wanted to do but never got around to. Success means a new beginning, a continued but transformed involvement in life.

Success Teams are great for older people because they're an antidote to loneliness and isolation, and also to the boredom of passing one's time playing cards or watching TV. In a team, people don't just relate to each other as bridge or golf or gripe partners, but as unique thinkers, dreamers, and makers who can inspire each other. The richly varied interests revealed in a team pull the outside world back into the retirement community, home, or senior center, surrounding everyone with an atmosphere of activity and life. I'd also like to see some systematic way of making seniors into teachers in our society. They have a lot to contribute, and I think, given a way, they would gladly do so. What makes Success Teams really different from most recreational programs for senior citizens is that the activities aren't presented to the group by the counselor, but chosen and initiated by individual seniors themselves. They're not just passive consumers of services, or spectators; they're in charge. And that's empowering, at an age when the chief cause of depression and decline is the loss of control over one's own life.

The counselor's job is:

—to start up teams by running the two team-building exercises (p. 108)
—to guide the goalsearch process, encouraging team members to rediscover lifelong interests, talents, and loves
—to help brainstorm ways around physical limitations (e.g. finding talking books or volunteer readers or making arrangements for transportation for a would-be student who is visually impaired)
—to facilitate access to outside resources, from art materials and tape recorders to visiting speakers, performers, or teachers
—to encourage team members to view their children and grandchildren as a resource network (family members are usually happy to be drawn into a creative project, and families may become closer)

For that matter, there doesn't always have to be a counselor or recreation director. Enterprising senior citizens can start their own Success Teams, using this book as a guide. I'm so convinced that the years after retirement are an undiscovered treasure trove that I'm beginning to research it already and may make it an integral part of my next book.

This is just a sampling of the settings in which Success Teams can be used to connect and empower people. You could run teams in mental hospitals, in prisons, or as an adjunct to twelve-step sobriety programs—Alcoholics Anonymous and its offspring, including Narcotics Anonymous, Overeaters Anonymous, and Al-Anon. (One woman who belongs to both a twelve-step program and a Success Team says that their one-step-at-a-time approach is very similar: "Start at the beginning, know where you want to go, realize that there are lots of little steps to get there, and all you have to do is the next step that's in front of you.") Dream Teams are now running in government offices, just the same way corporations use them. Springfield, Illinois career educator Jane Shuman runs Success Teams especially for small-business owners. Teams could be a blessing to the dependents of American military personnel stationed abroad. They could be a whole new way of running singles' organizations—get together over dreams, instead of drinks. I'm giving you a tool that can be used in a thousand ways, some of which you will invent. Whether you work professionally with other people's dreams or just privately with your own, I hope you'll take the basic theme of Success Teams—putting team spirit and support behind individual aspirations—and improvise.

That's what the rest of this book is all about.

PART III
VARIATIONS ON A TEAM

Picasso had to learn classical anatomy before he could draw a woman with both eyes on the same side of her head. And I had to show you how to run a basic Success Team before I could invite you to take the concept and play with it. Now it's time to play—to discover the multitude of different ways that the principle of teaming up for personal dreams can be put into action to enrich your life. I will tell you about a dozen bold departures from the standard Success Team design that people have created to fit particular needs and resources. These stories have only one purpose: to inspire you to come up with your own ingenious variations on a team. (And I hope you will write to me and tell me about them.)

The basic team, as you know, is four to six friendly acquaintances working on four to six different goals. But you can also team up with just one other person (The Buddy System, p. 182); you can make your family into your team (The Home Team, p. 187); you can form a short-term team in which everyone shares the same goal (The Job Club, p. 192; Kick-the-Habit Clubs, p. 198; The Create-an-Event Team," p. 194); or you can join forces with people in your own field to teach or learn the ropes (Mentor/Apprentice Teams," p. 208), or to make more professional progress than any of you could alone (Guilds, p. 201).

But not all of life is goal-oriented. You can also use the team principle as a new way to have fun, to learn things, to get to know new people, or to get together with old friends. The playteams described starting on page 211 are the dessert of this book. Boy (Girl) Scouts of America (p. 211) and The White Elephant Sale (p. 213) have only one purpose: to meet men (or women). The Culture Club (p. 214) and Town Meetings (p. 221) are for learning, and sharing knowledge or artistic skills. Sunday Brunch (p. 221) and Cafe Society (p. 222) are open gatherings of friends at which anything can happen. These teams are for company and pleasure, but they also help to build the ultimate support system: a community of friends who turn to each other for ideas and advice and learning and laughter.

VARIATION 1: THE BUDDY SYSTEM

The buddy system is a mini-team of two people who make a pact to work together to meet both their goals. Kids at camp go into the water holding hands, scuba divers never go down without a partner, and I firmly believe that when you enter a new element in life—whenever you "get your feet wet" or "put a toe in the water"—you deserve to have at least one person looking out for you.

Remember the very first team instruction in this book: Tell a friend? The buddy system builds on that basic act, creating a structure that guarantees reciprocity (the fair exchange of time and help) and accountability (you know someone's waiting to hear what you did on your project). Like a Success Team, your buddy is your appointed conscience, your brainstorming partner, your auxiliary resource bank (two networks are better than one), and a hand to hold when you need one. Does it work as well as a team? It's different. In some ways the buddy system works better, in other ways not as well.

Advantages of the Buddy System

—It's easier to find one buddy than four teammates (especially if you're very busy, or very shy). You could start a buddy system tomorrow.

—A buddy is almost always a good friend. A team can be made up of strangers, but the buddy system is too intimate for that. And so you have much more access to a buddy. You can usually call him or her any time, day or night.

—It's easier to coordinate two people's schedules than five. And two take up less space. So finding times and places to meet is less of a hassle.

—There's never too little time at your meetings.

Disadvantages

—Fewer brains for brainstorming.

—Fewer hands for barn-raising.

—The group energy is missing. If one of you is down, it's hard work to pick him or her up.

—Absences don't just shrink your team, they wipe it out.

—It's harder to keep meetings structured and businesslike.

—The dark side of unlimited access: a buddy in crisis may either demand too much of your time, or get too little help (four people can provide a level of support that one person can't). The buddy system is ideal for people who live alone, who don't have other sources of support or competing claims on their attention.

The real deciding factor will be your own preference. Success Teams have more energy and resources, but they're a bit less intimate, and harder to start and run. And if you don't like groups, all the advantages of a five-person team won't persuade you. The Buddy System gives you many of those same advantages in the context of one-on-one.

Meetings with your buddy follow the same format as Success

Team meetings: report in; brainstorming and barn-raising; plan and schedule next week's steps; switch. But there are a few differences:

Before you start to work together, be sure you're both very committed to your agreement. A Success Team can start out with six or seven people and whittle down to four or five, but in a two-person team there's no room for dropouts. (Note: it's easier to make and keep a firm commitment if you make it for a limited time period. Then, at the end of the three or six months or whatever time you choose, you can renegotiate and decide to keep going, or not.)

Commitment is also important from week to week. In a team you can let yourself slip for a few weeks, and feel good just helping the others. But a buddy system gets badly unbalanced if one buddy is working and the other one isn't. Schedule at least one midweek call to make sure your buddy is on track.

The clock timer, so vital to the Success Team, is irrelevant in the buddy system. You'd feel really silly talking to one friend for precisely twenty minutes. Since you won't be pressed for time at meetings, you can each take as much time as you need, as long as you maintain a sense of equality. Just keeping an eye on the clock will take care of that. However:

The start on time and limit socializing rules are more important, if anything. The intimacy and informality of two people together makes it very tempting to have a kaffee klatsch, sports report, or confession session instead of a business meeting. If you want to make progress toward your goals, draw a firm line around goal mode. Differentiate it clearly from social mode.

Depending on your relationship and your other commitments, make an agreement on how you'll handle crises. Is unlimited access okay? Or would it be better to set a maximum number and length (usually three minutes) for panic calls? Are there times and places where one of you should not be called, because of job or family priorities?

The buddy system works best with clear-cut goals, whereas a more structured Success Team can support one or two people who are searching.

The buddy system is a natural for two people who've been struggling alone with the same goal—to finish a creative project, to find a job, to exercise, or to start a business. "I just started running," Andrea R. told me. "I'd been avoiding it, and I knew that alone, forget it. So I called a friend who also wants to exercise, and said, 'Look, you want to go into this together?' We check in with each other almost every day. I get messages saying, 'Hello, this is the Keyes Exercise Clinic. Today I did such and so. How about you?' "

I knew two people who got their Ph.D. theses finished by getting together almost every day and writing in the same room. And, of course, students have always known the advantages of teaming up with a study buddy for homework or exam cramming.

Some very successful partnerships have been based on the buddy system design. When Andrea decided she wanted to sing for old people in nursing homes, she didn't want to do it alone. "I called up a friend who's a lot like me: she's classically trained, she's done a lot of acting, and it's really important to her to help people. When I asked her if she wanted to do it, she just screamed 'Yes!' We were meeting all the time at lunch because we worked at the same place. We'd have to get together whenever we took another little tiny step, and we'd get all excited. We discovered that we worked in very different ways. I like to work in a more formal way, whereas she's very informal. I like things regular, and she can deal with a lot of unpredictability. So it worked out that I did most of the nuts-and-bolts stuff—making the brochure, typing, writing letters nonstop, calling—and she supplied the confidence! At every stage there was a major obstacle, and I'd think 'Oh, there's no way we can do it!' and then she had the idea that got things going again, and we'd get through it. I don't think I could ever have done it all alone. It was great just having somebody to complain to who was on the same track, so she really knew the depth of the complaint!"

Friends working together in the buddy system can easily overcome one disadvantage of not having a team by throwing an idea/resource party or small-group brainstorming (Chapter 4) whenever they need more inspiration or contacts. "Right at the beginning Barbara gave us a resource party with seven or eight of her talent pool people," Andrea said. "We were there for at least three or four hours. They gave us a lot of ideas about making up a brochure. We talked about a name for the group—we didn't use any that came up then, but it put us on the right track. Somebody suggested videotaping a performance to show to people who were interested. They gave us a lot of detailed advice. It was great just knowing that was available; it gave me this feeling of how much you can get by networking."

Career and guidance counselors can also make good use of the buddy system. Those who work with a larger group or team for a limited time period often put group members into pairs, to add a dimension of intimacy to the group experience and/or to set up the ongoing support system that's easiest to sustain after the group ends. In high school teacher Sue H.'s Nyack Success Team (p. 164), the twenty to twenty-five students are paired off with planning partners who pledge to keep each other on track. LaVaun Maier has members of her support teams share their written reports on the past week's progress in twos before going on to the whole-group meeting. Melanie Keveles teaches the buddy system to her displaced homemakers' teams in Duluth: "It's a six-week group, and people get all geared up during the six weeks, but then they can lose their momentum. I think the buddy system is a good way of keeping it going. What I do is hand out buddy system instructions near the end of the group."

Career counselors who schedule working sessions with individual clients get a fee for being, in effect, an expert buddy—and a buddy who requires no reciprocal help. "I have about twenty-five clients now," says Jane Shuman, who is building a private practice in Springfield, Illinois. "They're people who want to change careers, both men and women, and they range from professional and managerial people, doctors and lawyers and bank vice presidents, to a coal miner, a man who runs a grain elevator, and a number of nurses and dieticians. I work with them one-on-one. I become their buddy, and they pay me for that instead of joining a Success Team. People make marvelous changes, and it gives them the courage to do what they love and not settle for less."

VARIATION 2: THE HOME TEAM

When I first invented Success Teams, I said they were a substitute for the ideal family we all wish we'd come from, but so rarely did: a family of winners who were glad when we won, who were so in love with their own lives that they'd happily help us learn and dare. I still think that a good family is the original Success Team—and that learning to work together as a team can make many families closer and better. It's a little tricky turning your family into your team, but I know it can be done, because my two sons and I have done it.

There's a sense in which every single parent already has a team with his or her kids. Single parents do something, of necessity, that most married parents don't do enough: they ask their kids for help. When you're the only parent around you have to delegate responsibilities to your kids and discuss decisions with them. This idea occurred to me years ago, one night when I looked around the living room and realized the kids outnumbered the adults. Your sons and daughters can be a fabulous source of support. I have never encountered saner, more considered advice than I've gotten from my own children, and other parents I've spoken to say the same. The children, in turn, get to feel needed and respected. As long as their needs aren't being ignored, they thrive on much the same thing a Success Team provides—the opportunity to give as well as get quality help.

By the same token, partners in a good marriage often say "We're a team," and many two-career couples act as each other's buddies, sitting down together in the evening to talk about what's going on at work and to brainstorm each other's problems. What the *Teamworks!* techniques can do is make you aware of the teamwork that's already happening in your family, and help you improve on it—by adding communication skills, so family members really listen to each other, and the inevitable emotional tangles and tensions won't sabotage mutual support. The place to practice these skills is in a Home Team meeting, which is carefully set apart—for very good reasons—from the rest of family life, but the beneficial effects usually spill over.

You'll get better at fighting, loving, sharing the Sunday paper, and getting the dishes done.

"The team really helped me with my children," said Virginia C. "When I first was divorced, I felt very guilty that I had done this to these poor children, and so I felt that I shouldn't require too much of them. I should let them recover. The team helped me to understand that they would recover better if they were part of the family team, and that I should definitely have them help me out, we should all be in it together. I instituted a family meeting that was not unlike my Success Team meeting. We did it every two weeks. We would parcel out the chores and talk about how things were going, how we could make them better, and what everybody wanted. I also let them take turns being the leader of the meeting. It wasn't just me. So it gave them a chance to feel that they were in the driver's seat."

Families can team up to meet both joint family goals—from routine chores to getting and training a puppy, building a rec room, planning a vacation, or starting a family business—and individual goals: ballet lessons, a car, a workshop, a skateboard, a scholarship. Some goalsetting guidelines:

—When you set a *family* goal, make sure that responsibilities are divided up very clearly, so that everyone takes charge of a fair share. People can choose the tasks they like best, or desirable and undesirable jobs can be rotated.

—Make sure that *individual* goals are really set by each individual—not by some other family member who thinks Sally should take ballet or Danny should be a Rhodes Scholar!

My younger son, Matthew, is my Home Team this year (after graduating from college and spending a year in Japan), and we have both joint goals and individual goals. He's my partner in a new business venture, and I'm his buddy when he has to get ready for job interviews. Living together creates special problems. Whenever we treat our business transactions with family informality—say he's sitting there talking to a friend and I zoom in and say, "What about the mailing list?"—we get into trouble.

But if I say, "Can we meet today?" he says "I'm free at two," and then there's no problem. I'm the same way. I want warning, not to be on constant call. Even more than acquaintances in a Success Team or friends in the buddy system, Home Team members need to draw a line around their business relationship, separating it from their everyday relationship, if they want to get things done without inefficiency and friction.

But habit and passion are strong. How can you keep the family jungle of emotions and behavioral routines out of the little clearing where you work as a team? There are a few techniques that really help, and they can be summed up in a few words: special time, special place, special behavior.

—Set a time.
   —Hold your regular Home Team meeting at the same time every week (or every other week).
   —If someone wants to call an impromptu meeting to deal with a problem on the spot, make an appointment, as I do with Matt. "What time will you be through studying? Can we meet in half an hour?" Always get an agreement to meet, instead of imposing on each other's time without asking.
   —If someone wants help with his goal in the middle of dinner, draw a line around it by raising a hand and saying, "I'd like to talk business for three minutes. Okay?" That's a request to shift to the team mode of talking and listening (see below).
   —If all you want from your family is advice, say so in advance. Families love to give advice. What makes them hesitate is being assigned unexpected tasks.

   —Change the setting. Whenever you want to talk business for more than a few minutes, go into another room— ideally, the same room where you hold weekly Home Team meetings. This is Matt's suggestion. He notes that when you change the setting, you're changing your relationship. So for an impromptu meeting, you might say, "When you're through with your work, I'll meet you in the kitchen." I prefer to meet in a room with a table, because each of you should also:

—Bring your materials—your calendar, note pads and colored pens, clippings, résumé, whatever. That helps you focus on your projects, rather than on personal issues.

—Use the team mode of talking and listening. In a scheduled Home Team meeting, this means that each member in turn is asked two familiar questions:
—What do you want? (or, What did you do this week?) and
—What's the problem?
In an impromptu meeting, the person who asked for the meeting can also use the two-part format to explain why. ("I called Mr. Johnson twice, but he hasn't called me back. What do I do now?")
The speaker, whether she is five years old or fifty, gets to talk while everyone else listens attentively. Listeners may ask for clarification but may not jump in with ideas or solutions until the speaker is finished. Then, ask one more question:

—What can we do to help?

The reason why talking in team mode is revolutionary for families is that family members are often bad at listening to each other. Parents have agendas and anxieties about their kids, so they rarely say, "What do you really want?" and listen to the answer. They're terrified that the kid might say, "I really want to be a Satan-worshipping heavy metal rock musician!" So instead of listening, they talk—"You've got to do your homework, because you've got to go to college"—and behind that is the unspoken fear ("or you'll wind up a homeless drug addict!"). It's true that the kid does have to do his homework. But when that's the only way parents respond to their children, children stop talking to their parents.

Teamwork creates a free space, apart from (not instead of) any necessary nagging, where completely different rules apply. Kids go to school, parents go to work—they have to do that. But team time is when they ask each other, "What do you want?'' and really mean it. Within the team, everyone is a peer. Nobody can assume that he knows what's best for someone else. Whoever is speaking directs the team; she can take a suggestion, reject it, or adapt it. She's not bound to obey.

Once families have gotten good at this on the safe ground of family goals and personal dreams, they can sometimes move into more dangerous territory—if they work at being honest. For instance, a parent might say, "I'd feel more secure if you went to college, but all I really want is to know you'll be all right." A kid might say, "I want to pass math, but the problem is I hate doing the homework. I guess you'd better pressure me. Don't listen to me if I fight back." Becoming a team doesn't abolish parents' authority or children's need and resentment of that authority. It doesn't make parents stop fretting about their kids' future, and it doesn't turn kids loose to do any fool thing they want. What it does is open a channel of communication so that both parents and kids can speak honestly to each other about their hopes and dreams—and be heard.

A Home Team meeting is almost exactly like a Success Team meeting, except that you may want to divide it into two sections—one for family goals and one for individual goals. When working on individual goals, use the clock timer religiously. It's very important that each family member gets the team's full attention for a full share of time. If you find you're having trouble listening to each other on occasion, try a variation on the Assets Feedback exercise (p. 111). Success Teams use that exercise to bring some personal warmth into a somewhat impersonal situation. Home Teams need to do exactly the opposite: bring some impersonal appreciation into a situation that's all too personal! Tell each one his assets, but don't talk about his good qualities in general—talk about the value he has for this team. "Matt always has good ideas. He's a good writer. Matt's a demon for work." "Danny's got nerves of steel. He's a great negotiator. He can say anything to anyone." That usually has the effect of bringing attention back to the meeting.

I find the only persistent problem we run into is overenthusiasm. My boys say to me, "You should quit work and go live in Italy." Matt and I always say to Danny, "You should put out another record. You're a great musician!" Danny and I always say to Matt, "You can get into any graduate school you want! You've got brains." We all say "We need another dog!" Sometimes it's hard to cool us down. But reason usually prevails, and most often I do not provide it, they do.

Most families can use at least some Home Team techniques to help them take care of family business and support each other's dreams. But there are families that can't swing it. They're either not close enough, or they're too close—like wrestlers. They can't back off and change roles. If you belong to one of those families, then the best thing you can do for yourself is get an outside Success Team, and the best thing you can do for your family is help them get teams of their own. Tell your wife to pull in her friends, and get your kids to team up with their friends.

Now we come to some variations on a team that break the rule about Success Teams being as diverse as possible. The people in these teams band together to do one of two things: achieve a goal they have in common (to find a job, stop smoking, create an event) or succeed in a common field—for example, they might all be writers or graphic artists—by cooperating, instead of competing.

VARIATION 3: THE JOB CLUB

The Job Club is a lot like the Success Teams that career developers run in outplacement and vocational rehabilitation (see p. 167), except that individuals can get together and start one for themselves. The idea had a very interesting beginning. Someone sent me an article about a priest in West Virginia who had read *Wishcraft* or seen me on TV and had been inspired to start a job club in his church. Every weekday morning he'd hold a meeting of all the people in his congregation who were out of work. They'd go through the want ads together, then go out in pairs and look for jobs. I thought that was a marvelous support system. I put a notice in my network newsletter: "Job Club Meeting." Fifteen people showed up.

Here's what we did. At the first meeting, we agreed that next time we met, all the club members would bring in any good career guidance books they had, tests they'd taken—some of them had gone through aptitude-testing programs—even questionnaires from magazines. Everyone would throw something in the pot. At the second meeting they shared all these materials, gave each other the tests, did the exercises from the books, and asked each other goalsearch questions (p. 36). The point was not to start looking for just any job, but to get matched to a company or a job description that would fit their personality and talents.

After that, everybody just operated like a team. They asked each other, "What do you want?" and "What's the problem?" Someone might say, "I think I want to work in international marketing."

"What's the problem?"

"I don't know exactly what's available, what one *does* in international marketing." The team would agree to help her find people in the field who could tell her what the possibilities were. Then we'd ask, "Any other problem?"

"I'm terrible at interviews."

"Okay, so we'll have to rehearse you. Do you know the companies to go to?"

"Yes, that I know."

Then we'd go to the next person: "What's *your* problem?"

"I'm phobic. I look at the want ads and I get depressed."

"Okay. Bring in the want ads next time, and we'll go through them with you. What else?"

"As soon as I circle something I think, 'I don't want to go.' "

"You need somebody to go with you. Any volunteers?"

And so on. Whatever a team member needs—moral support, valuable contacts, research suggestions, help writing a résumé—the team provides, just as in a regular Success Team. The only difference is that all the members of this team share one goal: to find jobs.

If club members are responding to want ads, they go out in pairs. Every job-hunting day two buddies meet in the morning to circle the ads and start making the rounds. You accompany your buddy to her appointments and wait for her downstairs; she goes with you to yours. When you come out of anything as difficult as a job interview, no matter how it went—good or bad—you've got to discharge the pent-up tension. You need someone to have a cup of coffee with and say, "I did great! I think I might have gotten it!" or "That guy's very tough. Do you know what he asked me? I think I blew it." Your buddy says, "You'll be ready for that question next time," and strategizes with you a little bit. With that kind of support, instead of giving up and going home, you can go on to the next interview.

The job club buddy system can even work for two people who want the same job. Each of you waits downstairs while the other goes up. Maybe your buddy comes down and says, "I don't think I got it. He's looking for someone with more accounting experience. These are the questions he asked. Go up there and give it a try—at least now you know what he's after." When you've both been interviewed, you cross your fingers and leave. If one of you gets the job, at least it wasn't a stranger! And maybe that person can find a way to pull the other one in.

For both results and morale, the job club is a tremendous improvement on the solitary struggle to find employment.

VARIATION 4: THE CREATE-AN-EVENT TEAM

This kind of team is well known to many of you—those who belong to organizations. But it wasn't known at all to me. It's called, "Let's get together and create an event." Members of organizations are accustomed to making remarkable events happen on a regular basis. But the rest of us, those who have never been on a committee, never produced a fair or a fundraiser, are unfamiliar with such miracles. Those of you who have produced events for your organizations might be inspired by the ingenuity of these teams who produce events for themselves.

I found out about this kind of team because some of them came into being for the express purpose of bringing me to town to give a seminar. These spontaneous teams were made up of individuals who decided that they wanted something and banded together to get it.

The first, a wonderful bunch of people I still stay in touch with after six years, is in Champaign-Urbana, Illinois. Two friends, Dianne M. and Helen P., read *Wishcraft* and decided that they'd like me to come to town to teach the things I wrote about. They'd never done anything like this before, but on *Wishcraft*'s advice, they pulled together other friends to help them out. All their friends were enthusiastic, not because they knew about me, but because they had never gotten together before to do a project.

This seed team was full of energy, strategies, and friendship. They pulled together a very impressive project, the upshot of which was that I came to their town to a seminar with over 175 people in it, and representatives from a number of businesses and organizations supporting the seminar were in attendance. But that's not the real story.

The real story is that bringing me to their town turned out to be a framework for getting together. They got the town paper to interview them and use their photographs. They went on radio. They spurred each other on, and in the process got to know and like each other more than ever before.

"Without this project, we'd never have had the excuse of working so hard together," said one. And another told me, "It was wonderful having you here, but all of us were afraid that once you left we'd stop meeting, because we wouldn't have any focus or goal." The star of that weekend wasn't me, it was that team.

The night before a Wisconsin seminar I met with the seed team at a dinner. They all had personal projects going and had started helping each other with them—that is, they'd turned into a Success Team and were helping each other attain their own dreams. But that night they decided to do something else as well.

"We work so well on a shared project, let's come up with another one," one of them said. "Not another speaker!" said another, "no offense, I'm exhausted." And then came a voice from the end of the table. A small, dark-haired woman said, "Why don't we all go to Paris next year?"

There was dead silence. Everybody looked at each other. "Hey," I said, "What about me? I want to come." They all smiled, but kept looking at each other, then smiled even more. And a new kind of ongoing team was born.

Springfield, Illinois, career counselor Jane Shuman created a team for the same purpose—to bring me to town for a Long Seminar—but her teammates were professional acquaintances rather than close friends. At least, that's how they started out. They're close friends now.

"When I decided I wanted Barbara to come to Springfield, I quickly did some brainstorming: who besides me would have a stake in wanting to learn how to make our wishes come true?" Jane recalled. "I wrote down the names of four or five women in town who were connected with organizations that might have some interest in the seminar: the state career guidance organization, Women in Management, the Junior League, the American Association of University Women. That afternoon I called those women, got them interested, and asked them who else to contact. I didn't decide the whole approach in advance and try to sell it to them. I said, 'Here's the rough idea. How do you think we could carry it out?' I got them involved in the brainstorming, so that they had an investment.

"The five of us decided that we would put on a breakfast and each bring something we made, coffee cake or donuts. We didn't have a budget—this is really a small town! So we sent out letters of invitation to people in forty organizations, and we also called those people, so that they had a personal follow-up. People from twenty or twenty-five organizations showed up, and we showed the video of Barbara on the Donahue show. [There's an idea here for career developers. Videotape yourself running a seminar, or appearing on local TV. A brief video clip is a great promotional tool.] We said, 'Here's our dream. How can we make this happen? Would you be willing to donate either time or money?' Out of that, we got a task force of ten to fifteen people. Another woman and I cochaired it, and we started meeting on a regular basis.

"I say 'task force,' but we called ourselves a Success Team with the goal of bringing Barbara to Springfield. We looked at the obstacles, brainstormed each step, and then drew up task plans and time agendas. We created an organizational structure to take care of arrangements and publicity, and we got a graphic artist to do the poster and brochure. We put up posters everywhere, and we had a mailing party for the brochures, with wine and cheese. People brought in the mailing lists from their organizations, so we had the two hundred members of Junior

League, and all the members of the American Association of University Women. We all donated the work, and it was really a lot of fun.

"Over two hundred people attended the seminar, and things have been happening in people's individual lives ever since. Some really close friendships grew out of this experience, as well as some good working relationships. That seminar was such a success that we actually had a profit of a couple of thousand dollars, and we started brainstorming what we could do for a second act!"

I haven't come up with a snappy name for this create-an-event kind of team yet, but I've suggested the idea to a number of groups, and heard from them later about wonderful things they did. They pulled ideas from the air—any idea would do, as long as it made everyone light up. One group hired a scholar to take them on a tour of medieval universities in Paris, Oxford, and Cambridge. On the cruise to Europe they read about Heloise and Abelard, listened to lectures on Dante and Aquinas.

Another brought a sailing club to their town by getting businesses to build docks and stores. And another team opened a playhouse, and puts on original theater pieces. I've heard stories of tennis instructors being brought to a summer home for a month, and a group of the owner's friends converging there to improve their games. One team started a writers' retreat by finding a local person with an estate who loved the companionship of writers. Now they're planning a photographers' retreat. Another team organized a trip to the Galápagos islands with a local scientist.

And I'm reminded of one of the earliest of these teams, the one created by long-lost friends to fulfill the dream one woman confessed in my first seminar.

Helena admitted she had a fantasy of living with her friends from years ago in a wonderful villa on the Riviera, and having everyone do wonderful things such as paint or write or play piano all day, then gather together for meals or to go out on the town. She knew all the people she wanted; they had been students together in Europe. When we asked what she needed, she said, "A million dollars." I never pay much attention to that answer.

Instead we made her call all her friends directly from the seminar. When she came back from the phone, she was flushed and looked stunned. Her friends loved the idea, were going to split the costs, and one of them would find a villa to rent within a week. All she would need was plane fare—and if she'd been unable to find that, we'd have thrown a ticket party for her and raised the money.

With a little help from your friends, imagination is liberated; farfetched dreams can become realities. With imagination and shared enterprise, friendship takes on a new dimension.

VARIATION 5: KICK-THE-HABIT CLUBS

The name of this one explains it. Team support isn't just a great help to people who are trying to break addictions; it's a necessity, as Alcoholics Anonymous and all its descendants (Narcotics Anonymous, Overeaters Anonymous, Al-Anon) have proven. These twelve-step sobriety programs are probably the simplest, most effective support systems in existence. But not everyone needs that degree of support to kick a habit. I've designed a couple of teams for people with everyday, garden-variety addictions, the kind most of us fight all our lives more or less ineffectually.

Variation 5a: Creativity Versus Bad Habits

This is a team I designed for a group of people who all wanted to lose weight, quit smoking, stop drinking too much, or stop being so disorganized—to cut out various self-destructive habits. The point was that at the same time as you quit smoking, went on a diet, got your life organized, or whatever, you also had to start writing a novel, or learning to act, paint, or play an instrument. The minute you kicked any habit, you had to fill the space with creativity immediately. I'm convinced that addictions are connected to empty spaces—the gap left when a person is avoiding the development of his or her deepest self.

With that conviction, I started a Success Team of people who all had twin goals: to get rid of a bad habit and to start a creative project.

At every week's meeting we'd report briefly on our progress at kicking the bad habit. The focus of the team, however, was on venturing into new territory. Starting at the second meeting, everyone would read aloud what she had written that week, show what she'd drawn or photographed, or play what she'd learned on her instrument. If she'd had any problems, we would brainstorm and offer support. We'd do everything in the world to encourage any creativity each team member had—help her get to a painting class, lend her a computer, recommend our favorite writing teacher, explain camera f-stops, suggest books to read. It worked miracles.

There's something about putting these two complementary goals together that makes both of them work better. Practicing the piano not only helps you lose weight; in some mysterious way, losing weight also helps you practice the piano. Maybe it's because they're both a total shock to the system. Both require a radically new way of operating in the world. You need no consolation prizes or cookies when you're functioning in a creative way and getting respect from others for your work.

A word about creative goals. If someone in the team can't choose one, have him or her write an autobiography. Or make autobiographical collages with family photographs. I know a man who does photo montages of his family. His visions of people are beautiful. You can do a visual autobiography—or a musical one, for that matter. But autobiography almost never fails to awaken creativity. It works so well that (for a variation on a variation) you could run a successful Creativity Versus Bad Habits team in which everyone did an autobiography of some kind. (Autobiography clubs are fun even if you don't have any bad habits—see Autobiography Salon, p. 218).

Occasionally, I encounter people who are not at all creative. They insist they're not, and it turns out that they're right. But I've found that people who are not at all creative are often athletic: they dance, run, or play tennis, and get deep satisfaction from it. If you encounter a person who is neither creative nor athletic, she probably loves to learn or to travel. Any of these goals are creative enough to replace bad habits.

Variation 5b: Procrastinators Anonymous

I used that name to get attention when I put an ad in the paper—and did I get attention. I've never gotten so many phone calls in response to an ad. I'm sure I would have gotten even more if it weren't for all those people who put off calling me. This is a Success Team designed for people who want to break one particular bad habit: procrastination. To be more precise, it's a Success Team that carries one Success Team feature—intensive care (p. 132)—to absurd, but effective, lengths.

Procrastinators Anonymous as I ran it was task-specific. Everyone came into the team with something he had to get done and kept putting off. Someone couldn't do homework. Someone else couldn't write a report, or do his taxes. Each person made a contract to stay in the team until that task was done. Then he could choose another, or leave the team until he needed it again.

Here's how it worked.

If someone, for example, had been putting off writing her thesis, the team would ask her to find a block of time that's available to her each day. Then teammates would decide who would call her at that time.

The next day at the appointed time, she would get ready to work. She'd sharpen her pencils, fill her coffee cup, and sit down at the typewriter. Then she'd get her start-up call: "Hi, are you sitting down?"

"Yes, I am."

"Good. Will you turn off the phone?"

"Yes, I will."

"Is your coffee there?"

"Yes."

"Very good. You will not get up from that chair until ten o'clock." And then, the key question, "What are you working on?"

Her answer would have to be specific: "I have to do a paragraph about the labor movement in Chicago." Her teammate would ask for more explanation and start her talking about the subject. Five minutes into the call, she *wants* to stop talking and start writing. Then the teammate arranges to call back at the end of the time period to hear how she's done, and hangs up. Once again, the little miracle happens when you drive away isolation. The idea that you'll be telling someone what you're working on accompanies you through the whole chore and makes it feel completely different. You actually look forward to the call.

Another technique you can use is what someone called the Curse of the Answering Machine. If someone in the team has five telephone calls to make during a time when no one is available to nag him, a teammate would ask him to report in to her answering machine. "At eleven o'clock call my machine and tell it who you're about to call. Afterward, tell it how your call went and who you're going to call next. I won't be there, but my machine knows everything, and it will tell me. If I don't get those calls, you're in big trouble."

Procrastinators Anonymous works almost every time. It works *every* time if you're willing to go the whole way. By that I mean sitting next to the procrastinator throughout the entire chore, even doing it with him. Kids will even do their homework if you're willing to go to such extremes.

I once provoked a procrastinating painter into working on a canvas she couldn't complete. I picked up a brush, dipped it in paint and started painting the canvas myself. It took about four seconds for her to snatch the brush out of my hand and get to work, mumbling insulting remarks about my ability.

VARIATION 6: GUILDS

The support teams or networks I call guilds (after the craft guilds of the Middle Ages, which were mutual-benefit alliances of bakers or ironworkers or scribes or other crafts people) are associations created so that people in the same field can join forces to help them all thrive. The secret of making a guild work is specialization for cooperation. If you're joining with others in the same field, you must carefully define what each of you does best. The guild then acts as a team to promote its members and expand opportunities in the field. As a guild, the team gets respect. It can contact prospective clients and get a call-back, which individual members might not. It can distribute jobs among members depending on each one's specialty. The result: more work for everyone—and more creative contact with colleagues.

So far, I've invented or encountered two kinds of guilds: one for private teachers or counselors who see individual clients, and one for craftspeople—carpenters, graphic artists, movie-monster makers—who command more clout and business in a network than alone. There are many other variations: Independent Scholars' Guilds, Graphic Artists' Guilds, and others I don't know of (but would love to hear about from my readers). Once you've got the general principle, you can figure out how to adapt it to your own field.

Variation 6a: The Therapists' Guild

I designed this guild for independent psychotherapists, but career counselors can use it, too, as can music teachers, holistic health professionals, tutors—anyone who works with people one-on-one in his or her own office or home.

Why do such people need a guild? Because the biggest problem in establishing yourself in any of these fields is finding clients. Advertising is anonymous—in a service so personal, clients hesitate to even begin with someone they've never seen or heard of. Word-of-mouth referral builds a practice slowly, over years. Meanwhile, clients are having just as much trouble finding you! Shopping for the right therapist or voice teacher is a laborious process that involves getting names from friends or the phone book, making appointments, and auditioning prospects one by one. A lot of people settle for a mediocre fit just because they don't want to keep looking.

I helped a group of fourteen psychotherapists form a guild that had as its main purpose to give each member exposure, a high enough profile to pull in clients for all of them. We met in my living room, where we designed the following program: They would form a panel and find speaking engagements. We came up with two topics, "How do you pick a therapist?" and "What's the difference between therapies?" We held a few meetings to work out what was distinctive about what each of them does, whose philosophies each espouses, how they choose to interact with a client. If their personal way of working didn't have a name—like Gestalt therapy or cognitive therapy—they made an effort to devise one. This would help the listeners to remember what they'd be saying.

I explained to the therapists that to make this panel effective, they—like any professionals who are accustomed to operating alone—would have to learn to operate as a team. In one of our first meetings, we had a rehearsal of the panel. I invited some friends, and we were the audience. The therapists had done a fine job of differentiating themselves and explaining their personal philosophies in the opening statements, but the question-and-answer segment created a havoc of competitiveness.

I improvised a new team-building exercise on the spot: touch football. We all went to the park and played football in two teams—the therapists against the audience. After half an hour, the therapists were handing off the ball, tossing and blocking for each other. We'd never have attracted any attention from the NFL—only one of us had ever played football before—but in one hour we learned how to pass the ball around and orchestrate a simple play.

When we got back to the meeting and ran the panel again, the difference was amazing. After one person had answered one or two questions, she would say, "I think so-and-so can answer that one better than I can," and pass it on. They realized that, in essence, this guild panel was a show they would be putting on, one in which they'd all have to come across well or none of them would, so they'd have to orchestrate it in advance.

The team brainstormed to find local groups in front of which they could speak—Parents Without Partners, Weight Watchers, the PTA, churches and synagogues. They decided not to charge any money since they'd be gaining visibility as the exchange for offering an informative panel discussion. Each of them would speak for ten or fifteen minutes, saying, "Here's what I focus on, and here's what I do best, and here's how I differ from other therapies." The contrast between the different points of view was truly fascinating. And when they all had spoken, they would invite the audience to ask questions.

I reminded them, "While you're talking and answering questions, something else is going on, too. People in the audience are getting to see what you're like. If anyone out there is looking for a therapist, he'll get to pick not only the therapy but the personality he's most comfortable with. After the panel is over, when you're walking around and socializing, people will walk up to you and say things like, 'I was very interested in something you said,' and 'May I have your card?' "

It works much the same way for other professions. You've just got to pick your forum. A bodyworkers' guild could go around giving talks at health clubs, in high-stress corporations, or to high school and college sports teams, explaining their different techniques for dealing with injuries, back problems, posture, and tension. A guild of five piano teachers might not choose to speak in front of the Garden Club, but I can see them putting on a show in the high school auditorium or the park, and advertising the event with flyers all over the neighborhood. If someone is looking for a teacher, seeing an ad for piano lessons is not the same as watching five people in a panel explaining—and demonstrating on the piano—their particular approach. "I like to work with adult beginners." "I only teach children." "I'm Vienna-trained, and I'm interested in people who want a concert career." "I teach jazz improvisation." "I teach sight reading." One teacher I know does brief demonstration lessons with a prize student.

One interesting thing about guilds is that they occasionally lead to business arrangements. A guild of therapists or bodyworkers might end up renting office space together, and opening a center that would attract more attention than any of them could alone. But most private teachers continue to work independently, by the very nature of what they do. The kind of guild I'm going to describe next is much more likely to metamorphose into a business, because members work in collaborative fields—like house renovation or moviemaking—where they have more credibility and versatility as a group, and can sometimes even be hired together to do different aspects of the same job.

Variation 6b: The Northern California Special Effects Network

The best part of having written *Wishcraft* is getting phone calls out of the blue from people who tell me how the book helped them change their lives. One of the most delightful calls I've gotten was from a young San Franciscan named Bill B., who started a network for special-effects experts that is fast becoming a nucleus of the film industry in San Francisco. What began as a support network soon became a guild, and it's now acquiring the capacity to act as a business entity as well. I think it's a real model for guilds in any collaborative craft. I'll let Bill tell the story in his own words—it's also a great success story.

"Since I read *Wishcraft*, my life has dramatically changed. A few years ago, I was sitting in a one-room studio in Washington State, with no money and no job. It was a really bad area, where the economy was seriously depressed, two major industries had gone under, and it was rainy and nasty and cold. I was dreaming of moving to California and becoming an artist, even though I had never done any kind of artwork except for one class in high school.

"Cut to the day last year when we wery lying around poolside at a very famous producer-director's mansion in Napa, surrounded by scaffolding and cameras, waiting for the sun to go down so we could do a night shoot on our first full-length feature film, with the mansion's owner as our executive producer. What a contrast! My feeling now is that anyone out there with a dream can make it reality. If I did it, anybody can—by networking. It's become my favorite hobby. I collect people now. It's the only way.

"Here's how it happened. Through networking with people I didn't even really know, I got moved down to California all expenses paid, and I worked my buns off for a while doing two jobs, and established a place to live. Ultimately I thought I wanted to be involved in movie special effects, and I worked on a couple of student projects. My involvement with that came from a friend who brought me an article in the paper about some students who were working on a film project with a creature, and the creature was in serious trouble. So I called them up and said, 'Would you like some help from an artist?' and they said, 'Yeah!' Ultimately that project was never finished, but a couple of us organized another group to move on to another project.

"By this time I knew how all the techniques are done, and I had high school students and college students coming to me and interviewing me for class reports on special effects. But I had a lot of trouble getting into ILM—Industrial Light and Magic—and the other places around here that specialize in special effects, even just to be interviewed. They were hiring people all the time, but it was impossible to find the avenues. It's an old boys' network. I was really discouraged for a long time. I finally decided to start my own network. I am the absolutely wrong person in the world to do it, because I'm incredibly disorganized, but nobody else was, so I decided somebody had to.

"About two years ago, I went to a special-effects symposium and workshop that ILM does every sixteen months or so. It cost $120 per person to go, and there were 975 people there, all fans, about half of them interested in pursuing a career in the area. I went in prepared with half-sheet flyers that said, 'If you had a good time today, find out more from the Northern California Special Effects Network'—which at that point didn't exist except in my own head. I had a couple of friends who were interested in the idea, and one gal, who was trying to help me become organized, had actually made up the flyers for me.

"The first wild thing that happened was I sat down in my seat—all the tickets were assigned seating—and sitting next to me was a short guy with red curly hair, and he had this photo album in his hands. I never like to go to concerts or whatever and sit next to strangers and introduce myself, but I started talking to this guy, and I said, 'Is that your portfolio?' He said yes. 'Can I take a look at it?' So I started looking through it, and he had built some fabulous creatures. So I said, 'Where do you live?' He said, 'I live over on the other side of the bay in Martinez.' I said, 'Really? Martinez is only about five minutes from my house. I love your designs, and I'd like to spend more time talking with you. This is what I'm really into.' And he goes, 'You're Bill B., aren't you!' Turns out that the taxidermist who I'd been buying my glass eyes from had been trying for a year to get us together, and out of 975 people in this symposium, we get seated right next to each other.

"After the symposium was over, about half the people stayed to look at the exhibits, and while that was going on I passed out about 500 flyers. And out of those 500, we got twelve responses, and three people actually came and found out what we were about, and out of those three, there's only one that still remains. Which was really discouraging to me. But in the meantime, something interesting was happening. I finally contacted the director of ILM. I had been trying to call this man for three years, and when I called up as Bill B., he never returned my calls. When I called up as the head of the Northern California Special Effects Network, he called me back in ten minutes.

"I said, 'Can you cast any light on why we didn't get more responses out of these people who paid $120 to be there?' He said, 'Well, this is exactly why we do not respond to individuals. We're inundated by fans who watch the films, see how fabulous it looks, and call up and say "Let me come sweep your floors and learn from you." ' These fans might have made some things that were really great, the director explained, but often it took them ten months to make them. ILM doesn't have the time or money or facilities to train them, or even to screen them to see which ones are going to last. Because anyone who's worked on any kind of film project will tell you that it's about 150 times more difficult and taxing, emotionally, mentally, and physically, than anyone would ever imagine. And a lot of people don't survive that initiation. So ILM's director saw the network as functioning in that capacity for them—screening people. That's a contact that we have not been able to utilize fully yet, but it's there for us."

Bill went on to tell me that in the meantime, the group that spun off from his first student project, plus a couple of network members, made—for all of $700—a thirty-minute video that they entered in several international competitions. One of them was the Sony International Video Competition in L.A. A well-known producer/director was the guest star judge, and he gave Bill's group first prize. When the video's director went to him and said, "How about some career counseling?" the producer said, "How about $100,000 and support backing to make your first feature?" So Bill and his friends made their first feature film.

The Special Effects Network now has about thirty members, fifteen or twenty of whom are active at any given time. Everyone pays a $20-a-year membership fee and does some volunteer work. Despite the name, it has expanded from being exclusively special effects to being an artists' network representing every aspect of art in film: screenwriting, mat painting, design concept. "I'm hoping to be the nucleus of the art department of the film industry in San Francisco," Bill told me.

In its present form, the network serves three purposes. First, it functions as a support network and educational system for young artists, professional and amateur, who want to find out more about their craft. In regular monthly meetings and other activities, the network brings artists together informally, so that they can exchange ideas about problems they're having, or new materials they're interested in and need to learn how to use. The network also serves as a clearing house for people who need its members' services. A two-page, full-color feature article in three major Bay Area papers not only increased membership but brought in some work opportunities. Bill hopes to expand this crucial function of the network. And finally, the network is talking about doing its own first independent project. "Except for administrative skills, we just about have all the pieces of the puzzle that we need to form a production company, raise financing, and make a feature film," said Bill.

Building on this model, I can imagine a guild of carpenters and contractors skilled in different aspects of house renovation, or a guild of theater technicians, or of graphic artists, or professional house-cleaners, or freelance book designers, or interior decorators.

VARIATION 7: MENTOR/APPRENTICE TEAMS

Getting started in any field takes talent, specialized skills, tenacity, and something else: know-how. The most promising young artist or entrepreneur still needs to learn how to market his or her skills, how to find opportunities and nail them down, how to approach the people with the power—agents, gallery owners, bankers. The usual way of learning these things is alone, by trial and error, which is slow, painful, and discouraging. There's a real need for both support and guidance— buddies and mentors. Mentor/apprentice teams provide them, and in the process, they provide supplementary income for seasoned professionals.

If you're a pro who has experience to share and would like to earn money for your expertise, you can run eight- to ten-week Success Teams for novices in your field, teaching them the ropes and also teaching them how to support each other. As usual, the best way to see how it's done is to talk to someone who's done it. Cynthia von Preid, a singer who recently moved to Phoenix, Arizona, ran Success Teams for singers in New York.

"Basically, it was helping young singers who came into town to cope with the adjustment," says Cynthia. "I set up groups of six to eight people, and we met once a week for eight weeks. I charged them $80, so it came out to about $10 a week. I knew they didn't have any money. They'd set goals individually, starting at whatever level they were at. But I wouldn't let them limit themselves in any way. I had them make dream posters. They had a week to come up with ideas and cut things out and make up their own posters of what they would really, really love to do, not what they thought was possible. That had an incredible effect on them.

"Then we'd go around the room and ask what each one needed to get done: find a teacher, get a picture, have enough nerve to call an agent and try to set up an audition—all the problems you encounter. Each week was something new, and we'd discuss what they came up against the week before. I would set up a buddy system if they had trouble, like anxiety over practicing every day. I'd have them do the telephone networking where they'd call and check up on one another, and then call back fifteen minutes later and report. That seemed to help them a lot. It went over really well, to the point where the Metropolitan Opera was sending people over. I loved doing it, and I still hear from some of those people."

You could do this is you were a racing-car driver, or an actor, or a painter, or a freelance writer, or a small-business owner. If you enjoy working with people, take a look at some area in your life where you are experienced and can offer good advice, and then start an ongoing team in it. Cynthia cautions, "You really have to know the ropes. You can't bluff your way through it." But it isn't a class, where you lecture at the front of the classroom and when they have their data, they go home. It's a mentor/apprentice team. You're a part of the team as well as its teacher, and you work with them every week.

For instance, if you were a nonfiction writer, your apprentices would bring in their material and read it out loud to each other. You'd show them how to make it better, and where you thought they should submit material. You'd help them find appropriate projects, tell them how to approach an editor, and share some of your contacts with them. A rare opportunity for them in this do-it-alone society of ours; a small business for you.

But enough of business. No more meat and potatoes. It's time for dessert.

I hope you've noticed that the line between work and play —or thinking and feeling—isn't very clear in this book. Success Teams are fun, whether they're helping you move toward career goals or personal goals. And getting what you've always wanted in life certainly makes you feel good. So why do I call the last teams in this book dessert? Because they have no other goal but to make you feel good. Unlike Success Teams, these playteams are not designed to help you produce anything or achieve anything or get anywhere. They are dedicated to enjoying life in the company of wonderful people. Another way to look at it is that Success Teams are for getting things *out* of you that are hidden inside—the thin person hidden in the fat person, the novelist hidden in the accountant—while playteams are for getting things *into* you that are delicious and good for you: stimulation and friendship.

VARIATION 8: BOY (GIRL) SCOUTS OF AMERICA

I hardly have to tell you that without somebody to love, a companion, the richest life can be lacking. Yet, as I discovered during the ten years between my two marriages, it isn't so easy for compatible single men and women to find each other. Leery of personal ads and sick of singles bars, I called a group of my buddies with a great idea: a way to meet men—and not just any men, but our kind of men. (In all honesty, my great idea didn't work, and you'll see why. But it *could* have, and I give it to you so you can take it further than we did.)

We called ourselves the Boy Scouts of America, and we even had an official Boy Scout sign, donated by one teammate's mother who worked on the children's floor of a department store. (It's a maddening fact that men seem to have less trouble finding women, but men tell me it isn't ever easy to strike up a conversation with an attractive stranger. I suspect that Girl Scout troops just like our Boy Scouts would get great results.)

Here's what we did. We wrote up a leisure-time activities questionnaire. It asked these strategic questions: "How old are you?" "What do you do for a living?" "Are you married or single?" "What do you do weekends?" "What do you do evenings?" "What do you do on vacations?"—in other words, just about everything you'd want to know about a likely-looking man. We were going to pretend that we were doing research, or writing a book, on leisure-time activities (which just happens to be a major at more than one university, in case anyone should question the legitimacy of the subject). And then we brainstormed places to go where the men we'd like would be.

The first place we met was in the cafeteria of the New School, a New York City university with one of the country's best adult-education departments. We got ourselves looking very official, with clipboards and pencils and bunches of questionnaires. We checked the class schedule for the classes where we thought the men might logically be, such as engineering and mathematics. And then we went out in pairs, because we were cowards. I think that actually made it better. The more embarrassed you are, the less you intimidate people and the more they want to help you out. We waited until they were coming out of class, and we walked up and said, "We're doing research on leisure-time activities, and we wonder if we could interview you." We interviewed about three men that first evening, and then we went up to the cafeteria and collapsed in laughter, gasping, "I can't do this anymore!" But the men were wonderful. They were flattered and helpful. They *loved* it!

Our next brainstorm was to take our questionnaire to the movie lines of our favorite directors, such as Woody Allen. We knew in advance we had something in common with the men in that line. We'd interview them while they waited for the movie. If a man said he was married, we'd just thank him and go on to the next one. But if he was single, and we got the right answers, and enjoyed the interaction, we'd say, "Can I call you if I have any more questions?" The idea was that if you liked someone you'd call him up, meet him for lunch in a public place, and get to know him better. And if you fell in love and wanted to get married, then you would tell him that you lied. And if you never fell in love, well—then you would write a book on leisure-time activities! It was one of my best ideas.

We did some brainstorming about all the circles of people in our town that we'd probably never get a chance to meet: the college professors, the architects, the musicians, the computer programmers. Then we brainstormed ways and places to meet them. I felt that we all tend to use up our own circle of people after a while, and need to locate new ones. With the courage and ingenuity you get from a buddy or a team, you can venture into many other worlds you otherwise might not. Look in the paper for special events, computer club meetings, poetry readings. Go prepared with a buddy or three and some questionnaires of your own devising.

So, were the Boy Scouts of America a smashing success? Yes. Did we all fall in love and get married? No. On that score, to be frank, we were a miserable failure. And the reason was that we had so much fun together that we kept forgetting that the point was to look for men. We'd interview a few, go to a coffee shop for a break, start laughing, and talk all evening. Sure, we needed men to love, but what we hadn't realized was how much we needed friendship time with each other. Having this team project had given us an excuse to get together. Once we realized that, we eased off on our man-meeting activities before they'd really had a chance to bear fruit. But the early results were very promising. If you start a Boy Scout troop, I can guarantee you that you'll have fun, whether or not you meet the love of your life on a Woody Allen movie line.

Here's another team scheme for meeting men that has had spectacular results. Somebody else designed this one—a genius, I think, who was far more results-oriented than I.

VARIATION 9: THE WHITE ELEPHANT SALE

A white elephant, as you may know, is a charming but useless object. At white elephant sales, people sell (or trade) their own white elephants and buy other people's, because what's useless to one may be precisely what the other needs. This concept became the basis for the absolute best way to meet mates that I've ever seen.

The idea was originated by the wife of a very successful psychiatrist I knew (in fact, it's how she met him). Twelve single women who wanted to meet men got together and formed a team. They agreed to have a party once a month, taking turns at each person's house. Everybody would cook something delicious, and help serve. And here is the smart part: each woman would invite to the party those men that she knew and liked, but didn't want for herself: the guy down the hall; the friend from the office; the sweet guy who was interested in her, but who she wasn't particularly interested in; her ex-husband or ex-lover(s), if she was getting along with them; her single cousins and brothers. These were the white elephants: likable but (from *her* point of view) useless men who might be just what someone else needed.

It turned out that everybody actually knew a lot of men, and of course no one felt at all shy inviting guys she wasn't romantically interested in. The men outnumbered the women three or four to one at these parties, but the men didn't mind at all, because the parties were great, the women were bright, energetic, and obviously resourceful, and the food was fabulous. Within six months, the team had a waiting list of 200 other single women who wanted to get into the group—and *six of the original twelve were either engaged, married, or living with men* who had been their teammates' white elephants!

What makes the white elephant sale work so well is that the men are preapproved and trustworthy—friends or relatives of your friends. But instead of fixing each other up with them on one-to-one blind dates—a tense and time-consuming way to interview romantic prospects—you create a relaxed, festive context in which you and the men can meet, mingle, and choose for yourselves. I've been talking this idea up for years, and once when I was about to be interviewed on the radio, the interviewer said to me during the commercial break, "So *you're* Barbara Sher! I went to a Barbara Sher party once." I said, "Oh! What's a Barbara Sher party?" and he described a white elephant sale! "Great party," he said. "I absolutely loved it."

Now I'm going to tell you about another kind of great party, which can be combined with a white elephant sale or run for its own wonderful sake.

VARIATION 10: THE CULTURE CLUB (SOIRÉES AND SALONS)

T. H. White, the author of *The Once and Future King*, had Merlin say to King Arthur, "The best cure for being sad is to learn something." I agree, and I would add, from my own experience, that the best cure for being bored and/or lonely is to learn something *with* somebody—preferably right in your own living room.

We normally think of learning or culture as something you go out and get—by going back to school, signing up for a class, or attending a lecture, play, or concert. Even if you go with a friend or two, you sit facing front, in an impersonal, public place, surrounded by strangers. From kindergarten on, in our culture, learning is separated from intimacy. And yet, if we eat together, if we feed our bodies in the company of friends, why not our minds and souls?

A few years ago, a friend was telling me about her new singing coach, a young unknown, who had improved her singing technique by making her understand all the words she was singing, even making her look them up in the German dictionary. I, who am permanently curious about everything I know nothing about, was intrigued by the thinking of her teacher and asked if I could come to one of her lessons. Then I got a better idea: ask the teacher if he'd come over and talk about opera. I'd invite people, let them bring $10 for him and food for the party, and we'd see what would happen.

What happened was the best party any of us had been to in a long time. The teacher, a young French pianist who had recently switched to opera, brought a singer to illustrate—gorgeously—his points, and explained to fifteen friends and neighbors what Beethoven's opera *Fidelio* was about and why it was great. We were entranced. When we broke for supper, everyone was in a marvelous mood. Practically none of the guests knew each other—I'd picked them because they didn't know enough about opera to argue with the teacher—but they were all warm and talkative after the lecture, and I was praised for being a great party-giver.

I love praise, and I decided if I could figure out how, I'd do another one of these things. Then one of the guests, a chiropractor, came up to me and said, "I love Beethoven, too. Let me prepare a lecture on the *Appassionata*." So there you are. It was meant to be. I got a volunteer to call everyone in my address file who didn't know a thing about Beethoven. Once again, a smash evening with talk, records, and lovely bits of piano playing. It began to dawn on me that I was hosting a modern version of *soirées*—like the ones held for eighteenth-century French aristocrats who used to gather, usually in the home of some formidable hostess, for evenings of music or discussion. If your soirees are held regularly enough—ours were shaping up to once a month—you've got a salon. We called ours The Culture Club.

Our next guest teacher was an amazing man who took us into the inner workings of the odes of John Keats with Sigmund

Freud as a guide. Everyone is still talking about that evening. Somebody's parents in their seventies, a pair of really smooth ballroom dancers, held a soirée in a dance studio where they brought their old 78s and taught us all to dance! I was a guest speaker, too, at a spinoff soirée, where I gave a talk on the psychology of creativity. I enjoyed preparing that talk more than I expected, because I never prepare talks. It gave me a chance to think about the issues at leisure, to research and study, unusual pleasures for me.

Afterward someone asked, "Do you think you can be creative and work in a corporation?" I said, "I don't know. Wallace Stevens did it, but I've personally never known a poet who worked in a corporation." Someone else said, "*I* know a good, published poet who works for a Fortune 500 company! I'll call him." For our next soirée, we invited that poet. He read his work, which was fascinating to all of us, and he explained how he keeps his soul alive and still makes a living. (We took notes.) At our latest soirée, my friend Lisa, a former actress who discovered that what she really loved was working with large primates, gave a slide show on her trips to the rain forest of Borneo, where she studied orangutans.

What do you want to teach? What do you want to learn? Start your own Culture Club and open up new worlds. Any member of your Culture Club (also known as your network of friends and their friends) can initiate a soirée. Maybe there's a topic that member is especially curious about. Maybe she or he knows a fabulous teacher, performer, or eighty-five-year-old friend with stories to tell who'd be willing to come talk to you, or sing/play for you, to teach you something about jazz or opera or Europe at the turn of the century. Or maybe the club member himself is an artist or performer—amateur or professional— and would love an intimate, supportive audience for a poetry reading or recital rehearsal. (It's a great way for a performing artist to prepare for a more intimidating public performance— and also a wonderful way to share private work that was never meant for the public.) Or maybe she or he has a passionate amateur enthusiasm to share, like Lisa's orangutans. Everyone brings food or drink and (if the teacher or performer can use it) $5 or $10. The evening's featured guest gives a presentation in the middle of a small, warm circle of interested people, and your other guests get to feel like participants, not spectators. Afterward, ask questions and have a free-for-all discussion. It's my favorite kind of party.

When I got too busy to organize the soirées every month, opera singer Cynthia von Preid took over. (She's since moved to Phoenix, and missed the soirées so much she's started giving them there: "The first one was a girl who's interested in dolphins and whales, and she gave a talk on marine mammals. People are fascinated.") Cynthia's Culture Club was not only a monthly feast of learning, but a salon and support group for creative people. "We had poetry readings. A girl who was about to give her debut recital in Alice Tully Hall gave it first in my living room. I sang at one of them. Another friend is a writer, and he wanted to get motivated to start a novel. So we gave him deadlines, and told him he had to come in and read something to us, even if it was just two sentences. Sure enough, he got very inspired."

Anyone who's ever tried her hand at creative work knows that it can be the loneliest work there is. You often wonder if what you're doing is great or terrible. To grow and flourish, creativity needs to be nourished, and the best nourishment comes from people who are interested in you. "You wouldn't believe the support and the real love that was present in those groups," says Cynthia. "When you throw a bunch of creative people together, there's an unspoken bond, a camaraderie. Never once was anyone critical in any negative way. You didn't have to prove yourself. You just had to share yourself, and the rest of us were there to listen."

Carla K. of Nebraska felt the need for that kind of support when she quit her administrative job at a radio station to live a more flexible, creative life. "I felt uncomfortable with friends who were in the nine-to-five mode and didn't understand what I was doing," says Carla. "I wanted the support of people who felt the way I felt. So I started talking about it to my hairdresser, whom I've been seeing for years. She's also an artist, a very creative person. I told her about your soirées, and she thought it was a great idea. We're planning our first one now. It will be a social gathering to meet like-minded people supportive of our artistic goals and lifestyle, and we'll also focus each meeting around a presentation. Each of us is going to invite five people and ask them to bring someone, so that we'll meet people we don't know, and we'll have fifteen to twenty people. I've already invited a friend who's a flutist, and another who works for a video company and is a musician on the side."

Carla hopes to build up a support salon of regulars. "The only problem is that I'd love to do it at a set time every week, but for a lot of people that's too much time commitment. My father used to belong to a Knights of Columbus group that met the second and fourth Tuesday of every month. That was nice, because even if they couldn't come, they knew it was going on, and if they couldn't make the second Tuesday they'd make the fourth. Maybe we'll do it that way. We've also thought about always meeting in the same place, so that people could just show up. [See Open Space, p. 222] There was an underground cafe where we could have met very comfortably, but it's unfortunately closed. So we'll start by doing it in her home first, and in my apartment the next time."

More variations on soirées:

Play readings. Groups of friends used to do them back in the fifties, but we seem to have forgotten how much fun they are, besides being a jolly way to find out what's so great about Shakespeare.

Reading circles. I belong to a Dante reading circle that's a spinoff of an especially successful soirée. We actually got together every other week and read *The Divine Comedy* from beginning to end. Then we were driven to read Virgil, because Dante thought so much of him. Now we're getting ready to read Virgil's hero, Homer. You could do exactly the same thing with Iris Murdoch. Or Winnie the Pooh. Or Stephen King.

Autobiography Salon. This is a wonderful one—very simple and almost endlessly rich. Every week (or every other week), each person writes a small piece of autobiography and reads it out loud at the meeting. And that's it. Have no fear that you'll run out of material; there's a seniors' group in San Francisco that's been doing this every week for *six years!* "M. W., retired nurse, is a member of the S. F. Scribes, 12 elders who meet weekly to share autobiographical writings," reads a notice in *The Idealog,* the journal of the San Francisco Brain Exchange. "When the group began six years ago its six charter members had limited writing background. They developed cohesion and trust through exploring and sharing life stories." That's not surprising, according to psychologist James E. Birren, Ph.D., director of the Institute for Advanced Study at the Andrus Gerontology Center, University of Southern California, who has taught autobiography workshops to people of all ages. "I have found that writing about our own life experiences and sharing them with others is one of the best ways we have of giving new meaning to our present lives by understanding our past more fully," Dr. Birren wrote in *Psychology Today*. "You understand your life better if you share it piece by piece with other people . . . Something happens during the reading that goes beyond what is achieved by the writing alone . . . New associations arise from the group discussion . . . Other people's experiences become reminders of feelings and events that we have set aside and thought we had forgotten . . . as each new session builds on previous sessions." The result is not only greater self-understanding for each member, but a strong bond between members. Many participants in Dr. Birren's autobiography workshops have "exchanged addresses and promised to remain in touch. Some members of [these] groups have had reunions to update their autobiographies."

In an autobiography salon, you can write whatever you wish each week, but it often works better to give yourselves group assignments for inspiration, so that everyone is writing about "My First Memory" or "A Special Place" at the same time. "Autobiography is most useful when it is guided," wrote Dr. Birren. "A good guide is like the old fisherman who always seemed to catch fish when others, with good equipment and the right bait, came back empty-handed. Asked why, he said, 'I know where the fish are.' " Some good fishing spots suggested by Dr. Birren:

—family history
—the history of your health and body
—how you got into your life's work
—experiences with death
—your loves and hates
—an early loss
—a broken love relationship
—your first crush

—your first job
—hidden pranks
—sibling rivalries

"Merely mentioning these topics can set off a train of rich associations," Dr. Birren wrote. He also suggested beginning by writing "two or three pages telling about your life as if it were a tree and describing its major branching points. Or think of your life as a river and tell how it flowed, taking a new path here and being dammed up there, narrowing and widening with events."

My friend Nancy Bacal in Los Angeles gives a wonderful autobiography-writing workshop in which the assignment is to write a four-part meditation on "The Hero's Journey." The four parts:

1. The Orphan
2. The Adolescent Boy (you should have seen *women*'s responses to this one, as they discovered the adolescent boy within them!)
3. The Wanderer
4. The Warrior

Dream Salon. I have heard of groups of friends who meet weekly to share their dreams—night dreams, the ones they have in their sleep—and to explore the life guidance, personal mythology, and symbolism in them. It's fascinating, because everyone starts remembering dreams very vividly, and sometimes group members borrow ideas from each other's dreams, or even have similar dreams on the same night!

To get your group started, read and share some good books on dreams, such as Patricia Garfield's *Creative Dreaming*, Gayle Delaney's *Living Your Dreams*, or Anne Faraday's *The Dream Game* and *Dream Power*. Each of you should start keeping a pen and notebook beside your bed, so when you wake up remembering a dream, you can write it down to share with your salon.

VARIATION 11: TOWN MEETINGS

Town meetings are gatherings of friends with a speaker, just like soirées, except that they're for discussing political and social issues, from the local school zoning referendum to whether Gorbachev is good or bad. Town meetings are a way to get informed together and have fun doing it. They can be parties with a focus, where someone who is knowledgeable talks on a topic that concerns everyone, and then opens the topic for discussion. Tap into your network. Chances are, you know someone who knows someone who knows . . .

—your alderman or city councilperson
—a political candidate
—an investment banker
—a Vietnam veteran
—an officer in the armed forces
—a social worker
—a volunteer who works with homeless people
—someone who's traveled to the Soviet Union
—a minister or rabbi
—a history professor

Invite any of these people to come and talk at your soirées. *Or:* one of your friends can read up on a subject she is passionate about, and give a presentation. Discussion should be frank and free-for-all—be prepared for it to go on half the night! Town meetings bring abstract problems alive.

An even less formal variation on town meetings was my friend Joyce's Great Conversations, otherwise known as the Sunday news and fondue meeting. Everybody contributed money, and Joyce would cook a fondue and great dessert and Irish coffee with ice cream. Everyone had read a news magazine during the week, and came to talk about the most interesting stories. They'd sit around the fondue or the Irish coffee for hours, talking. "We loved those talks," Joyce said. "We felt at that time that you could be well informed if you read news magazines, and that if a bunch of us did it and then had long talks and debates about issues, we'd be much better informed than if we were doing it alone.

"But the best part was just the level of conversation. I never realized my friends had such good minds, and I never got workouts like that myself, before or since. Also, now and then someone would bring a friend, and it was always someone we wound up liking, who then became a friend of ours.

"I don't think the get-togethers would ever have stopped, but everyone, including me, moved out of town. I really miss those times. I feel like my mind is getting muddy. I wonder if I could start a new news and fondue group without all those old friends."

She could. She knows a few people she likes, and they know a few others. She just has to put the word out and start small, and she should soon be back among her beloved great conversations.

VARIATION 12: OPEN SPACE

The last variation on a team is also the loosest—the most open and free. Open Space is a gathering that doesn't have a goal, a topic, or even a fixed cast of characters. It's just a regular time and place—every Saturday afternoon at a comfortable cafe, every Sunday noon in someone's living room—where people in your gang know they can come and hang out and find company if they feel like it.

It's a space where anything—or nothing—can happen. You might just sit around and drink coffee and read the paper; you might get into a great conversation; or you might find a new friend, a great vacation spot, or a used guitar in mint condition. Open Space creates possibility: the energy field that arises when people get together spontaneously and casually, without appointments or agendas. But that kind of gathering doesn't just happen unless there's a time and a place set aside for it—such as the cafes where European artists and writers used to find each other, or the central plaza of a Mexican town every Sunday afternoon.

We need Open Space because most of our lives are spent in boxes and tunnels. We live in houses or apartments walled off from our neighbors; we go back and forth along the same route to work every day; and when we want to visit our friends in their boxes, we make an appointment for a little slot in time, and write it in the boxes on our calendars. All these walls and schedules make sure that our lives stay on separate tracks. We don't get many chances just to flow together, pooling our minds and imaginations. Yet energy is created the minute we do find ourselves in that kind of situation. One fertile place for making new friends and connections is in the whirlpool bath or sauna of a health club! Among the jokes, the small talk and contented silences, people do brainstorming and barn-raising without even thinking about it. In the fifties in Berkeley, we drank pitchers of beer at Robbies and redesigned the world. After I left college, "grew up," and got married, that world seemed to disappear, and I missed it badly. So I re-created it.

Some friends and I thought up a kind of Open Space we called Cafe Society, or the Artists' and Philosophers' Coffee Break. Only one of us is an artist. But all of us have work of our own to do in the mornings—writing, studying, research-ing, making sales calls. We decided to locate a congenial coffee shop where we could hang out on an afternoon with a glass of wine or a cup of coffee. We agreed to have that be our open house. Every Saturday afternoon at two, we go there if we are in the mood, and usually find someone else. The catch is, we can only come if we've done some creative work that morning—but this is a very casual requirement. If you haven't done any painting or writing, all you have to do is a little philosophical thinking, and you're in. It's the honor system— you don't even have to report on what you did. But much of the time we talk about painting, about writing, about Plato or Derrida or ourselves, strenuous and refreshing talk, not easily found in everyday life. If anything it's better than college was because we're older and smarter.

A young editor I know coped with the loneliness of the big city by improvising an Open Space she called "Sunday Brunch." Her friends knew there was open house in her apartment every Sunday, from noon on. She provided fresh coffee and a Sunday paper; everyone who came brought something to eat—a loaf of bread, coffee cake, grapes, cheese. Any of them could drop by and bring their friends. It wasn't uncommon for six to ten people to show up, and some often stayed until twilight.

Having company in an unstructured way was the only reason for Sunday Brunch, so the editor was intrigued when other things started happening. People naturally talked to each other about what was going on in their lives, and as a result, someone found an apartment. Someone got a ride to California. Someone found a lover. Someone found a violin. Sunday Brunch was more than just a party. It was an Open Space. And an Open Space is a seedling of community—a kind of community that lives and breathes to help its individual members blossom.

I had a friend from Spain when I was a young mother living in Nevada. She got her house cleaned fast as a lightning bolt (I didn't), and then she would sit, elbows on the windowsill, and look at the empty streets.

"What's the matter with this country?" she'd say. "Where is everybody?" She told me stories of how it was to live in Madrid, where everyone walked out in the evenings, sat at outdoor cafes and met with their friends. "Americans are very sad, I think," she said.

That was in Reno, Nevada—gambling, Tahoe, fun. But casinos, floor shows, and glitter don't cover up a lack of contact in day-to-day living. She was right. Something's missing in our culture, and we're beginning to notice it and change it. Many of us are trying to speed up the process.

This book is my contribution. I want to hear about yours.

●●●

Index

227